MW01630488

K O L O R S

DAMIANI
StandardPRESS
PAUL KASMIN GALLERY

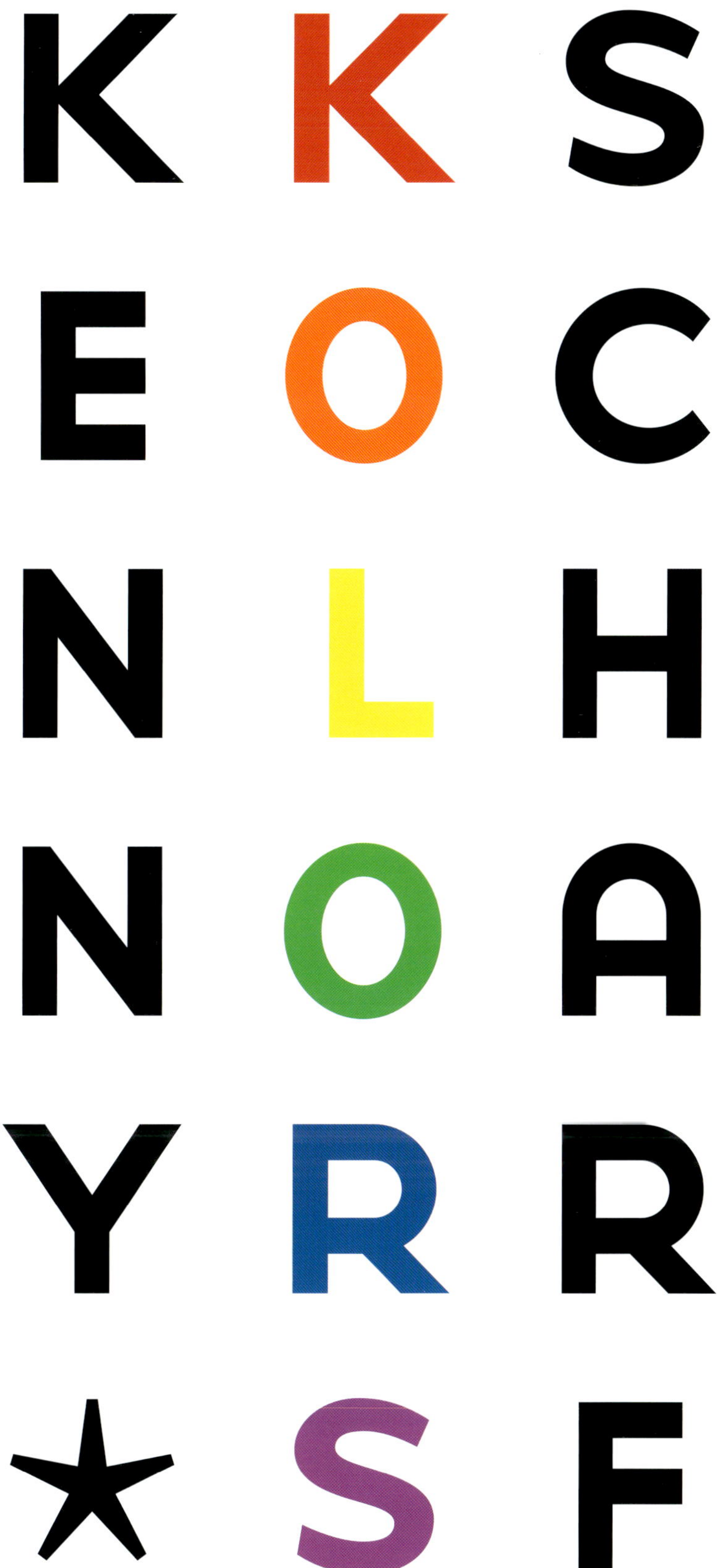

APRIL 4 - MAY 4, 2013

PAUL KASMIN GALLERY

FOREWORD BY JEFFREY DEITCH

"ONE OF THE GREAT OPTIMISTS OF FIN-DE-SIECLE AMERICA AT THE END OF ITS EMPIRE, KENNY SCHARF CONTINUES TO REMIND US NOW, AS HE HAS LONG INFORMED US, THAT ESCAPISM CAN BE VISIONARY PRACTICE, THE CULTURAL NARCISSISM CAN OFFER A SOCIAL MANDATE, AND THAT, NO MATTER HOW DREARY THE FACTS MAY BE, THE IMAGINATION (ALONG WITH SOME GLUE AND DAY-GLO PAINT) CAN ALWAYS OFFER AN ALTERNATIVE."
- CARLO MCCORMICK ['09]

"SCHARF IS, IN SHORT, QUITE THE MASTER OF DISGUISE: WHEN YOU HAVE FINISHED CATEGORIZING HIS WORK AS TOO MUCH OF ONE THING OR AT THE LOSS OF SOMETHING ELSE, HE HAS A TENDENCY TO SHIFT MEANINGS RADICALLY." - DAN CAMERON ['84]

"A LOT OF TIMES YOUR PAINTINGS HAVE A VIEW TO ANOTHER WORLD BEYOND THE ONE THAT WE'RE IN. LIKE SOMEONE'S MOUTH OPENS UP AND IT'S ANOTHER SPACE BEYOND THAT. EITHER EXPANDING AND GOING INTO SPACE, OR GETTING SMALLER AND GOING INTO MICROSPACE." - KEITH HARING ['85]

"THE ART OF KENNY SCHARF BEST EXEMPLIFIES A PARTICULAR TIME AND ATTITUDE IN RECENT AMERICAN HISTORY. INDEED, THE CONVERGENCE OF DIVERSE ARTISTIC, SOCIAL, AND ECONOMIC FACTORS HAD CREATED A DECADE THAT ALLOWED MANY ARTISTS TO THRIVE, AND THEY SEIZED THE OPPORTUNITY TO MAKE THEIR MESSAGE KNOWN. THROUGH HIS VISUAL EXPRESSIONS, SCHARF SOUGHT TO MAKE ART RELEVANT TO MODERN EXISTENCE AND TO OFFER JOY AND ENLIGHTENMENT WITH THE AIM OF CREATING AN IMPROVED SOCIETY." - RICHARD MARSHALL ['09]

"I LOVE THE SURREALIST. I COINED THE TERM POP SURREALISM TO DESCRIBE MY WORK. IT SUGGESTS THAT POP ART IS IN MY UNCONSCIOUS. IT'S LIKE BEING A SURREALIST PAINTER, BUT THE IMAGERY CREATED IS ALL POP IMAGERY. I LOOK AT MYSELF AS THE CHILD OF WHAT ANDY WARHOL WAS ABOUT. HE WAS PAINTING WHAT WAS AROUND HIM AT THE TIME. BUT SINCE I GREW UP IN THE '60S, I WAS LIVING POP. POP WAS MY WORLD. IT WAS INSIDE OF ME. OVER TIME IT BECAME A PART OF MY SUBCONSCIOUS, AND NOW IT'S FILTERING INTO MY PAINTINGS." – KENNY SCHARF ['95]

"WHENEVER ONE THINKS KENNY HAS REACHED HIS ZENITH, AND THIS GOES BACK FOR SEVERAL YEARS OF MY BEING FAMILIAR WITH HIS WORK, HE HAS YET ANOTHER SURPRISE IN STORE. I SIMPLY DO NOT KNOW HOW MANY TIMES I'VE SAID "HE'S DONE IT NOW. NO WAY HE CAN EXTEND AND GO FURTHER". FOR ME HIS CAREER IS ABOUT THESE EXTENSIONS AND SURPRISES." - IRVING BLUM ['13]

"SCHARF'S IMAGERY AND TECHNIQUE ADDRESS PROLIFERATION WITH A VENGEANCE; WHETHER IT IS LINKED TO THE ISSUE OF POST-NUCLEAR MUTATIONS OR NOT, HIS FIGURATIVE MODE SCREAMS OUT ACCUSATIONS (/AFFIRMATIONS?) OF CORPULENT ENNUI, MENTAL CLAUSTROPHOBIA, AND AESTHETIC GLUTTONY." - DAN CAMERON ['84]

"THIS NEW BODY OF WORK MARKS KENNY'S ACHIEVEMENT, MASTERING SCULPTURE BOTH CONCEPTUALLY AND FORMALLY. BY COMBINING THEM WITH THE MONOCHROMATIC PAINTINGS HE HAS CREATED A POWERFULLY COHESIVE EXHIBITION." - PAUL KASMIN ['13]

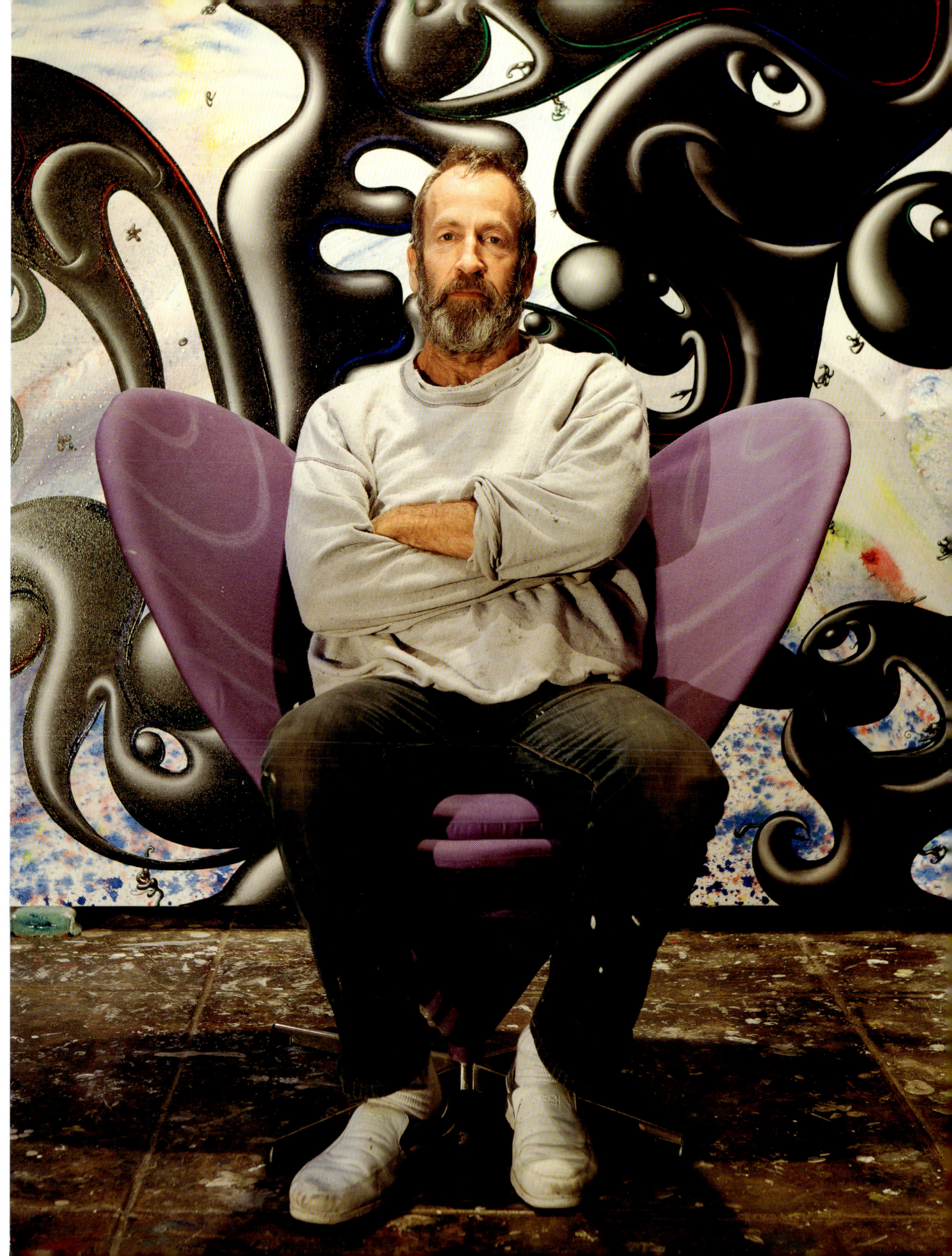

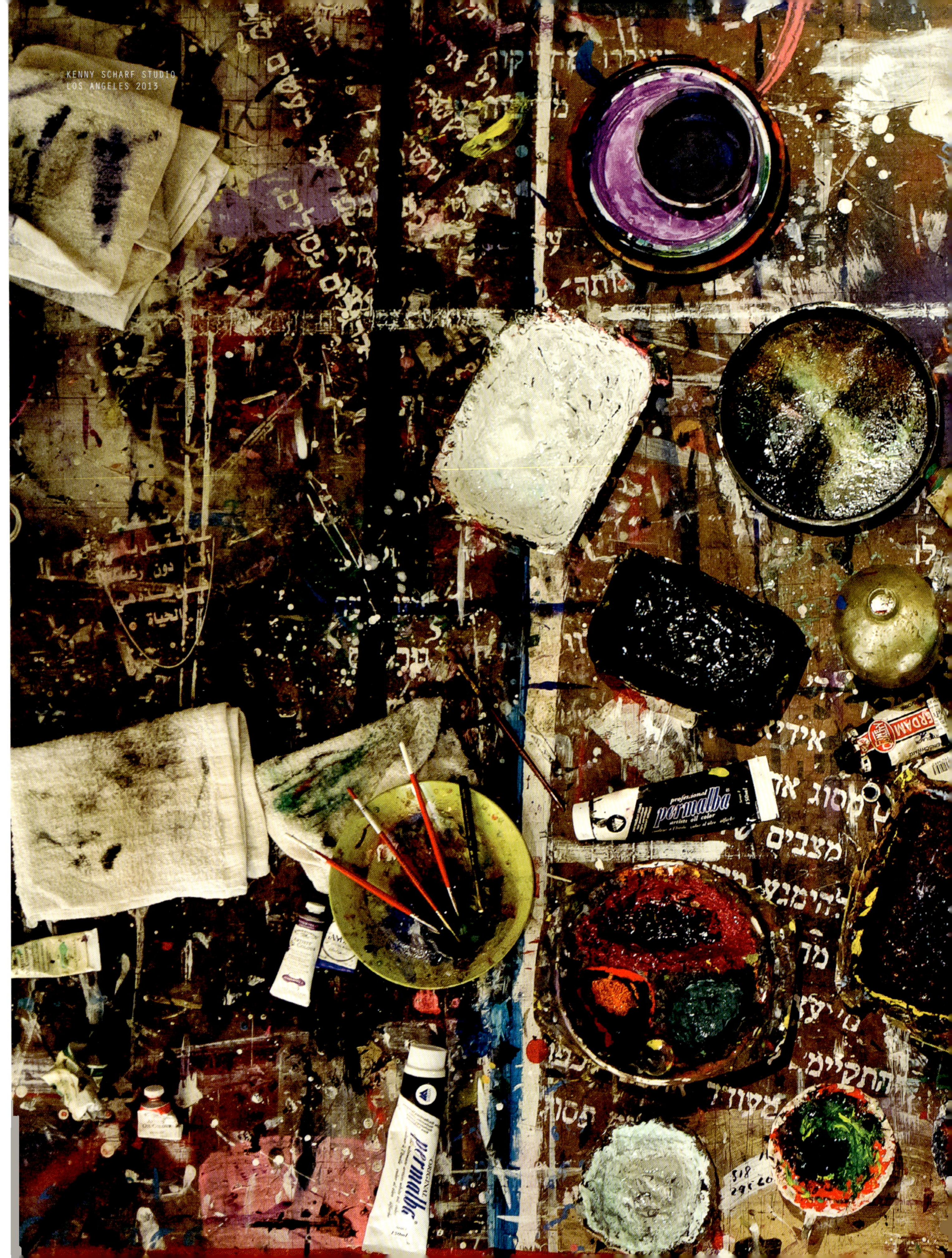

KENNY SCHARF STUDIO
LOS ANGELES 2013

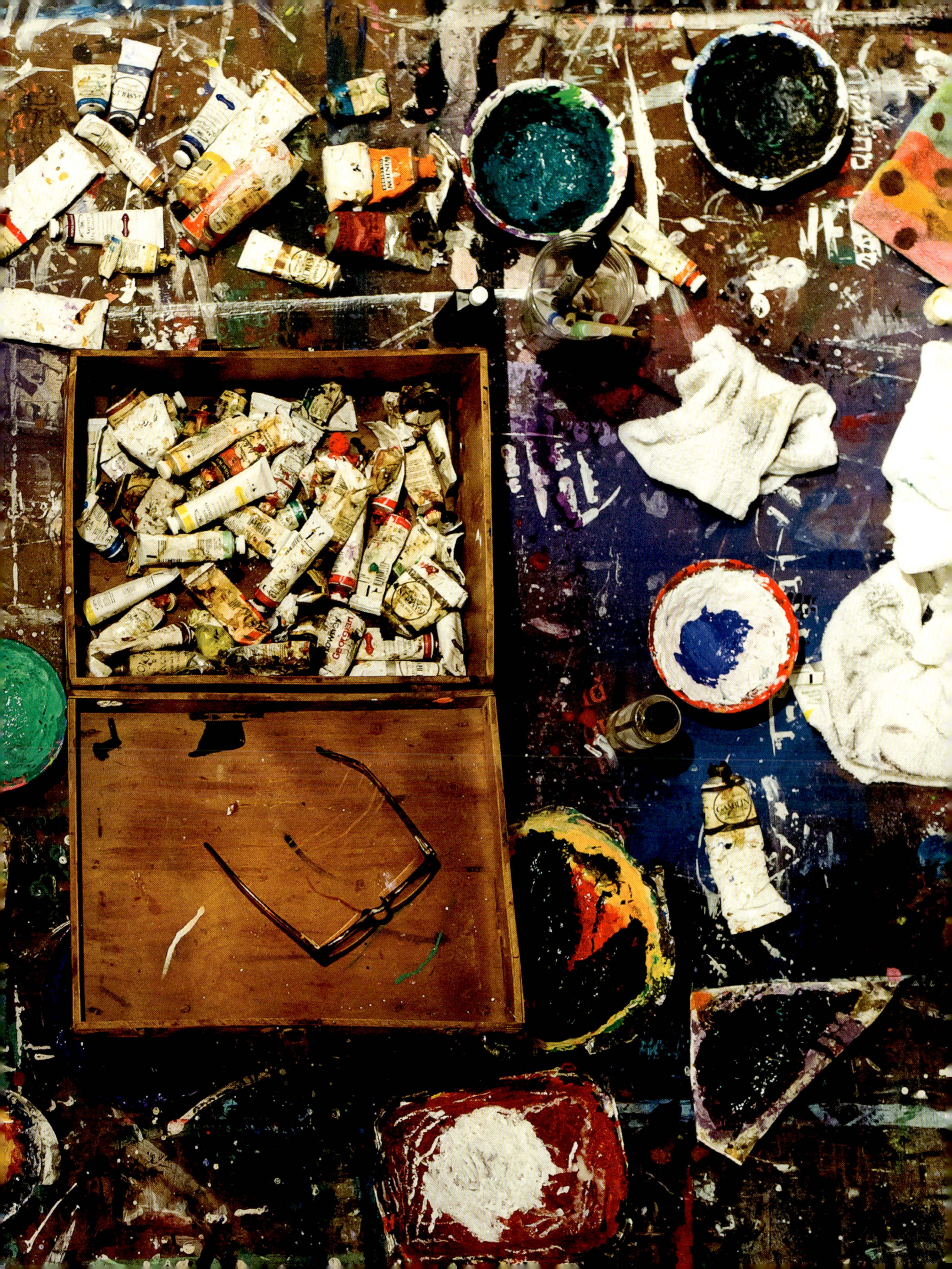
Georgian

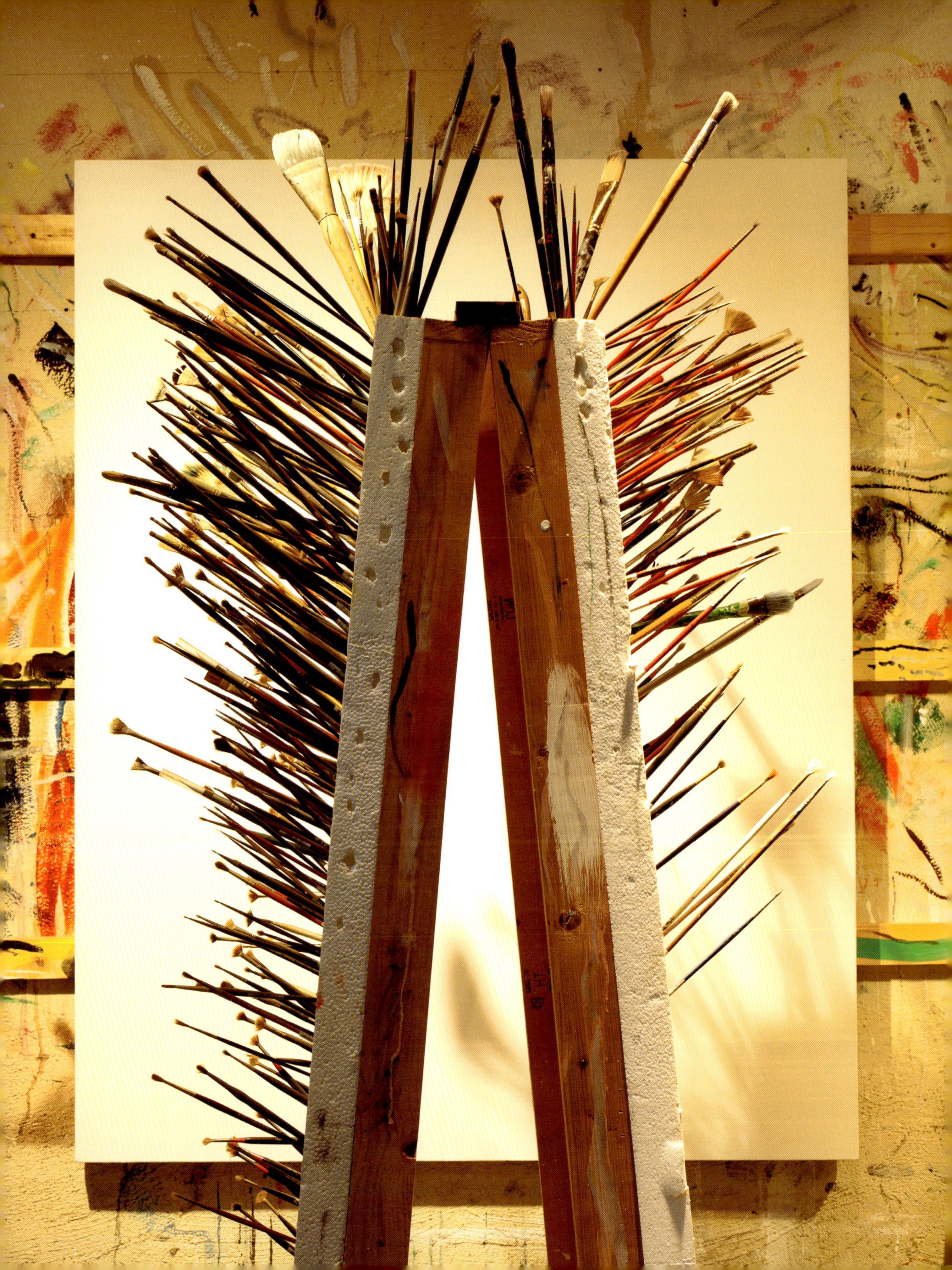

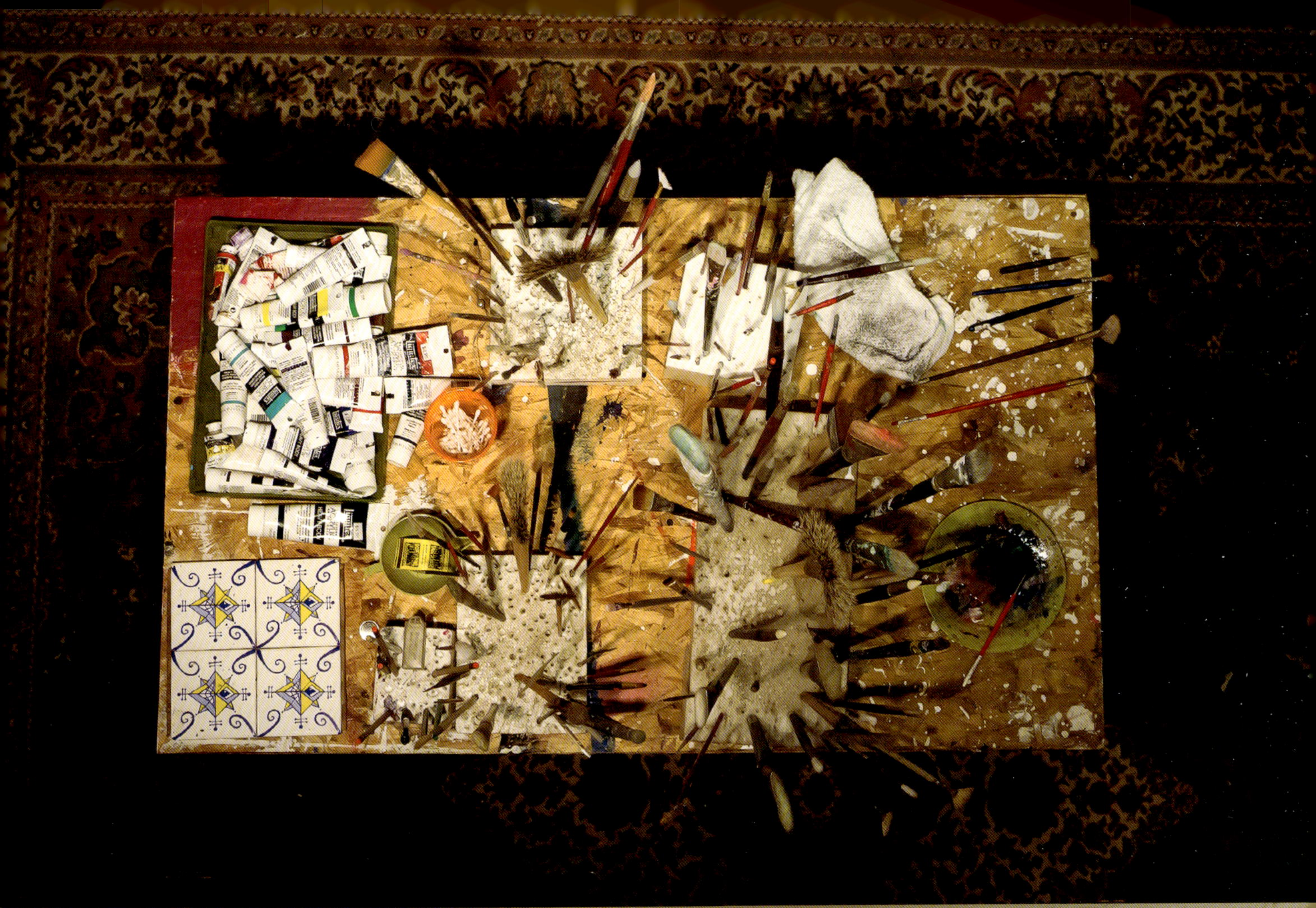

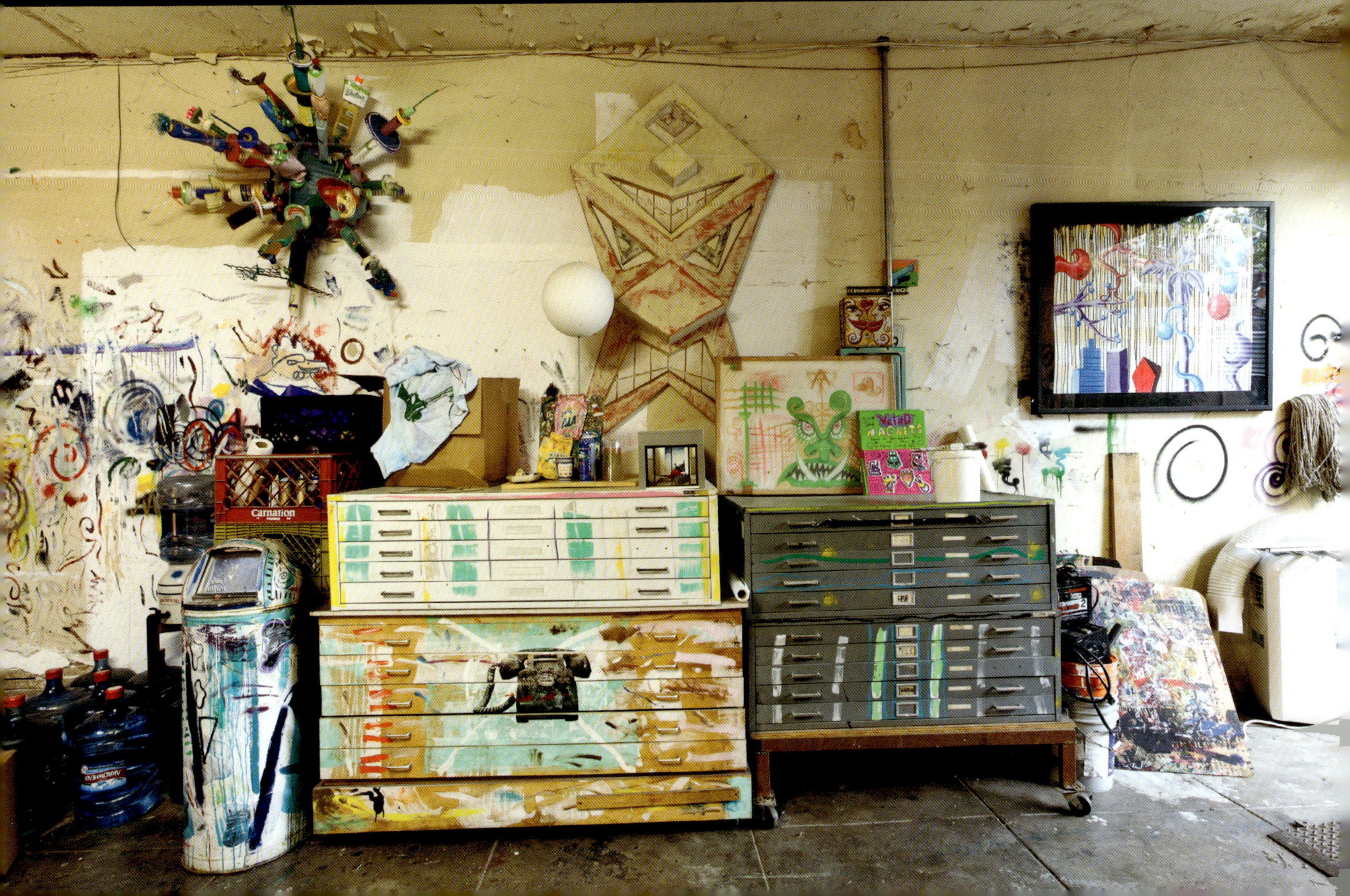

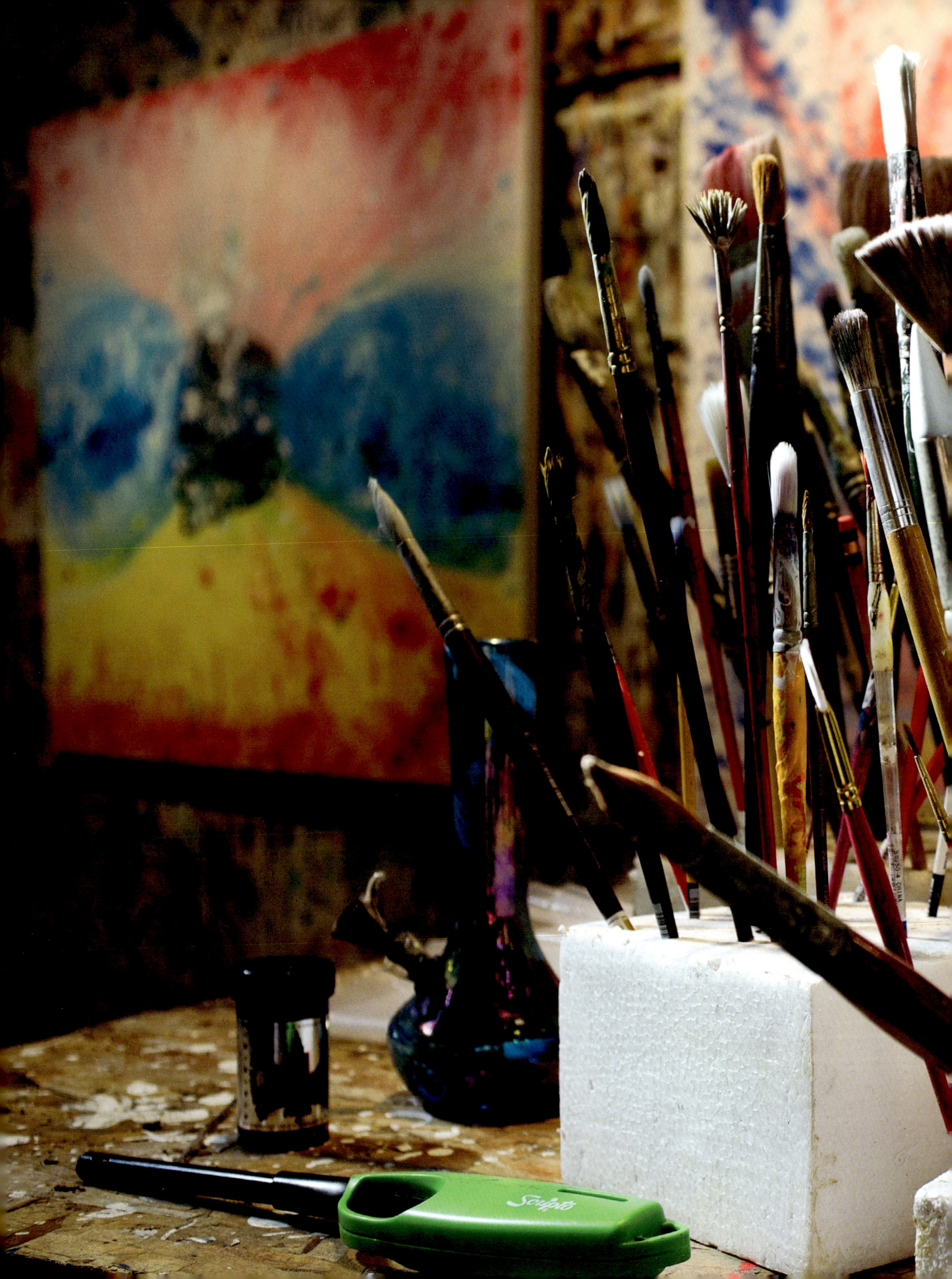
Scripto

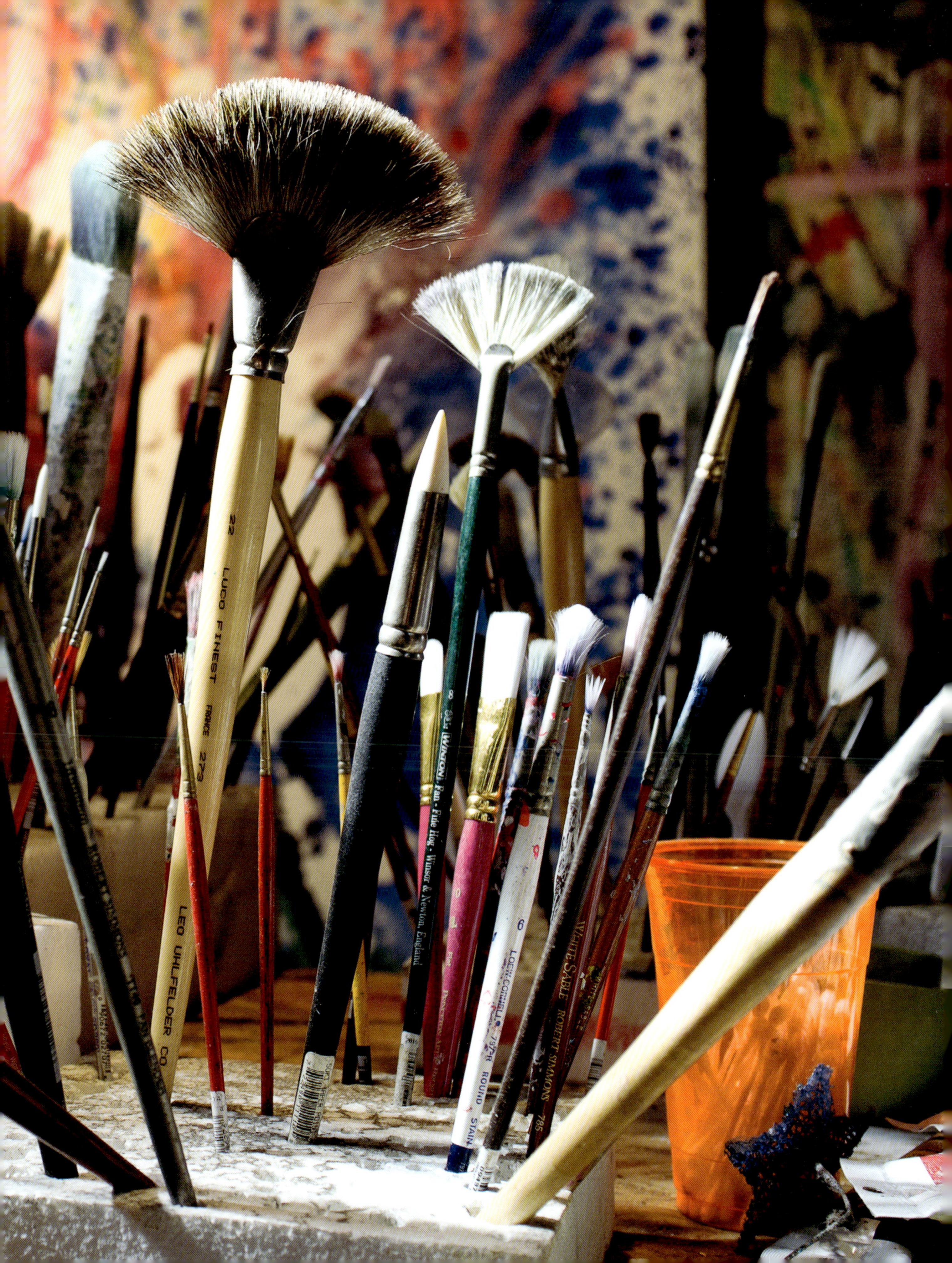
22
LUCO FINEST
FRANCE
273
LEO UHLFELDER CO
WINSOR & NEWTON
Winsor & Newton, England
LOEW-CORNELL
ROUND
WHITE SABLE
ROBERT SIMMONS

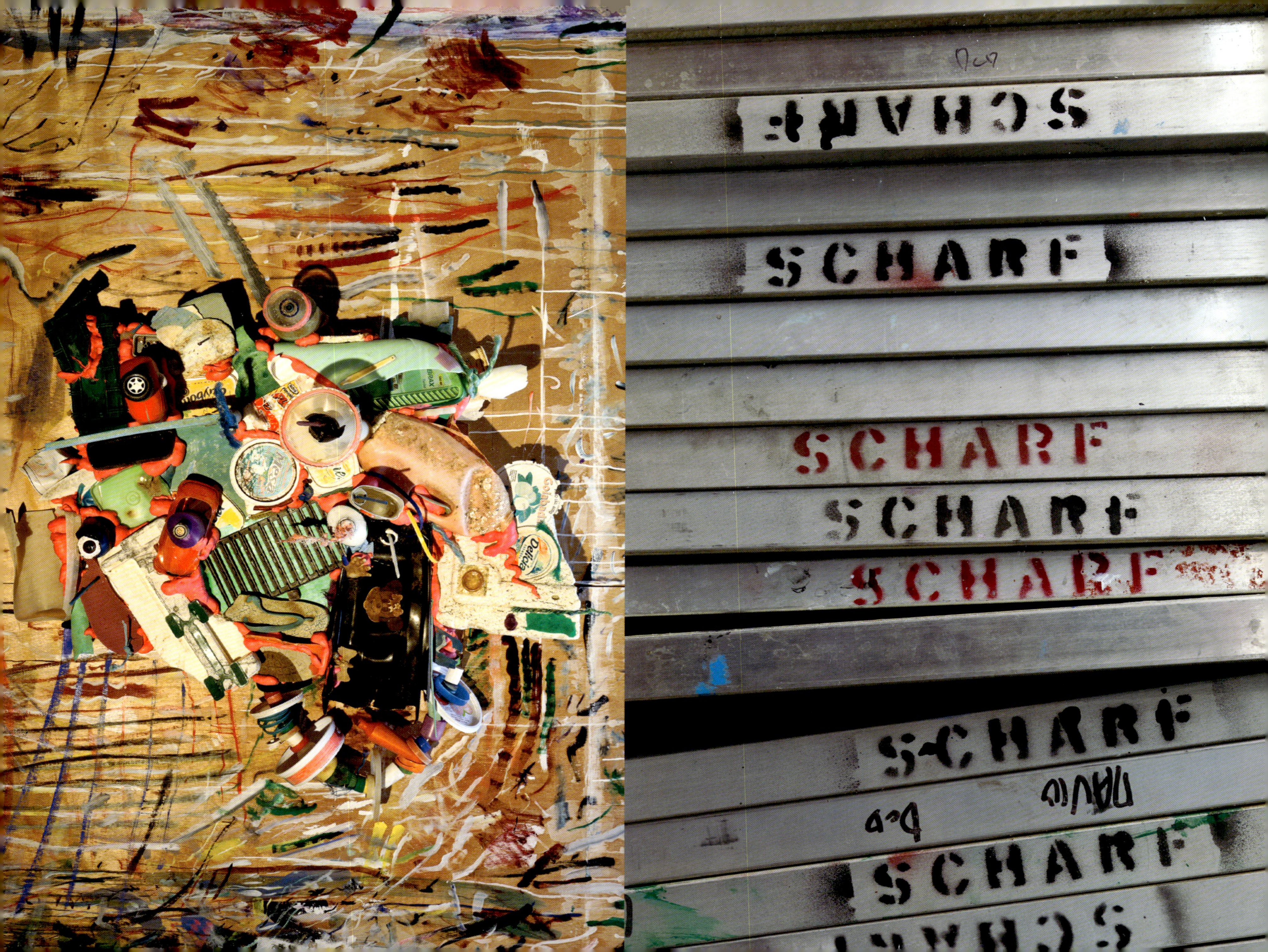
SCHARF
SCHARF
SCHARF
SCHARF
SCHARF
SCHARF
DAVID
SCHARF
SCHARF
BRAX
Delicia

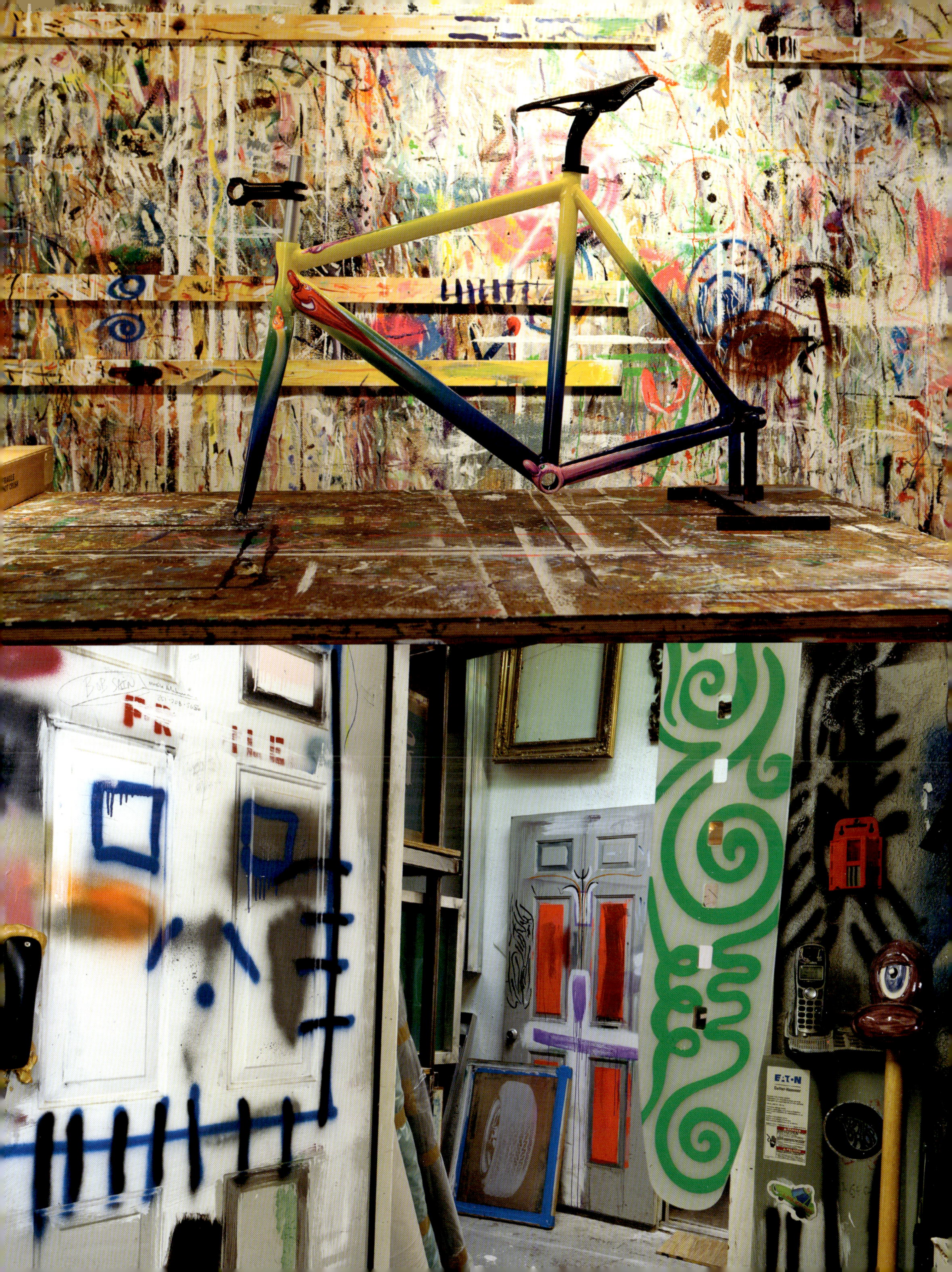
FR
ILE

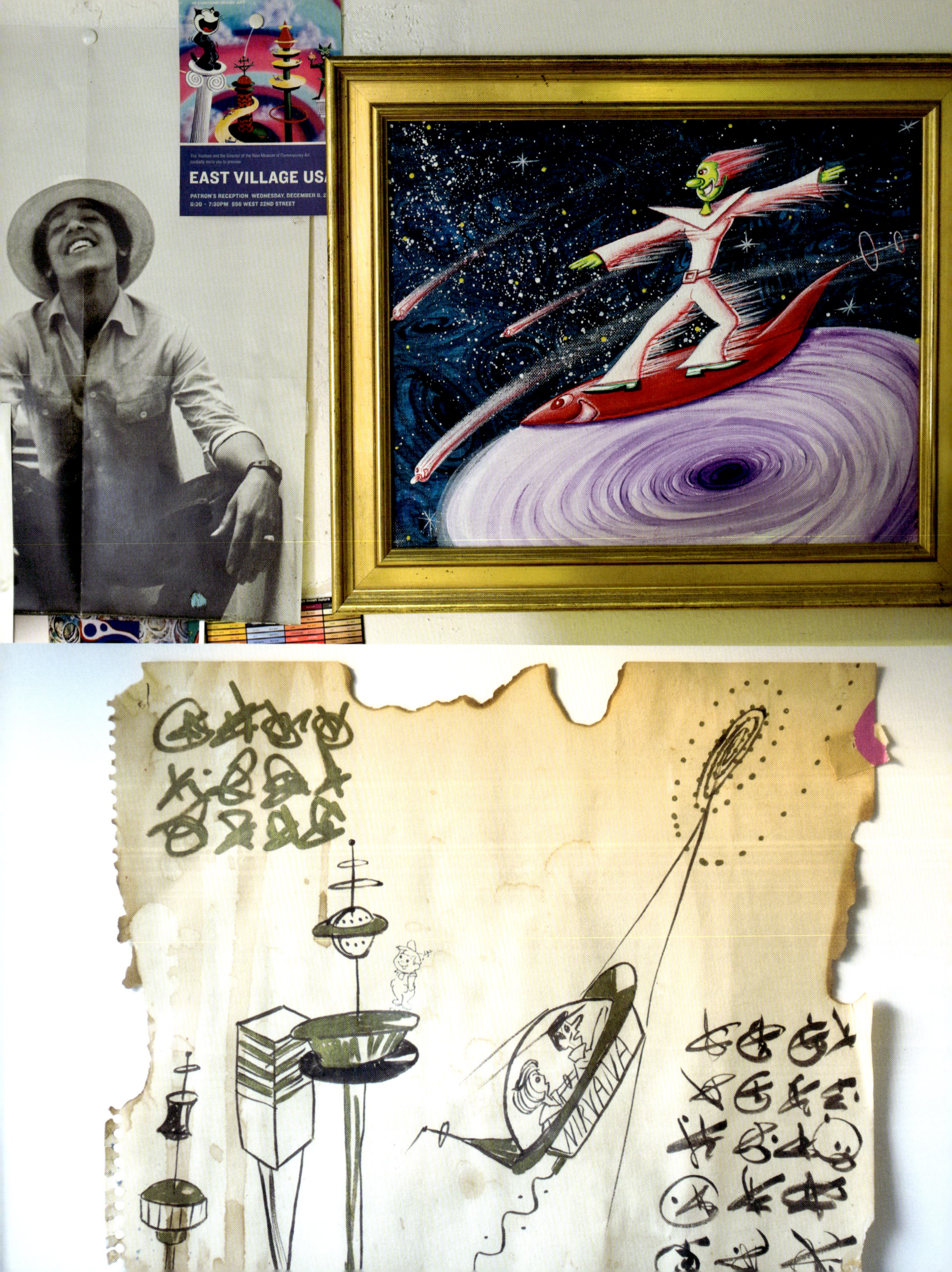
EAST VILLAGE USA
PATRON'S RECEPTION WEDNESDAY, DECEMBER 6, 2
6:30 - 7:30PM 556 WEST 22ND STREET
NIRVANA

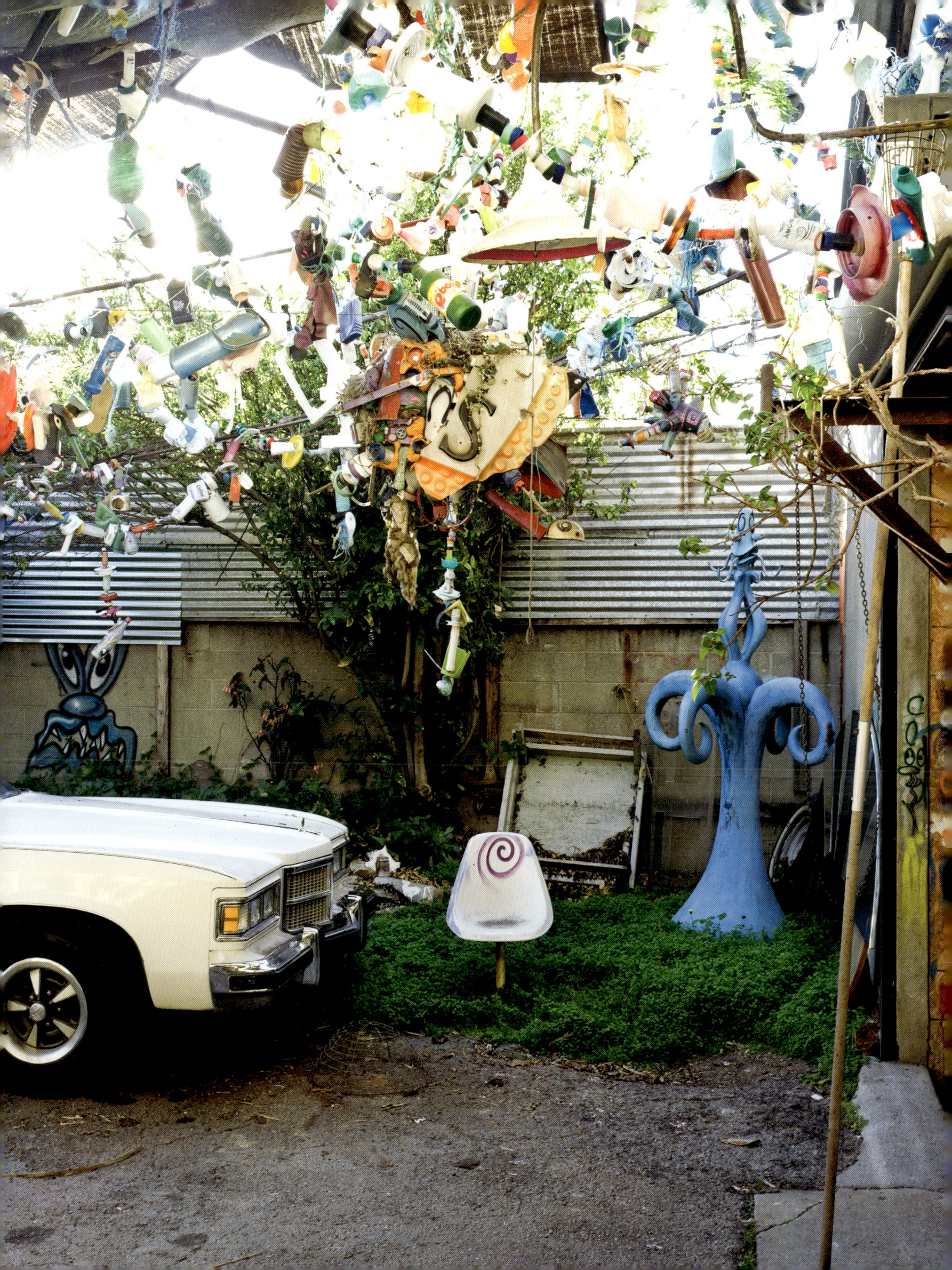

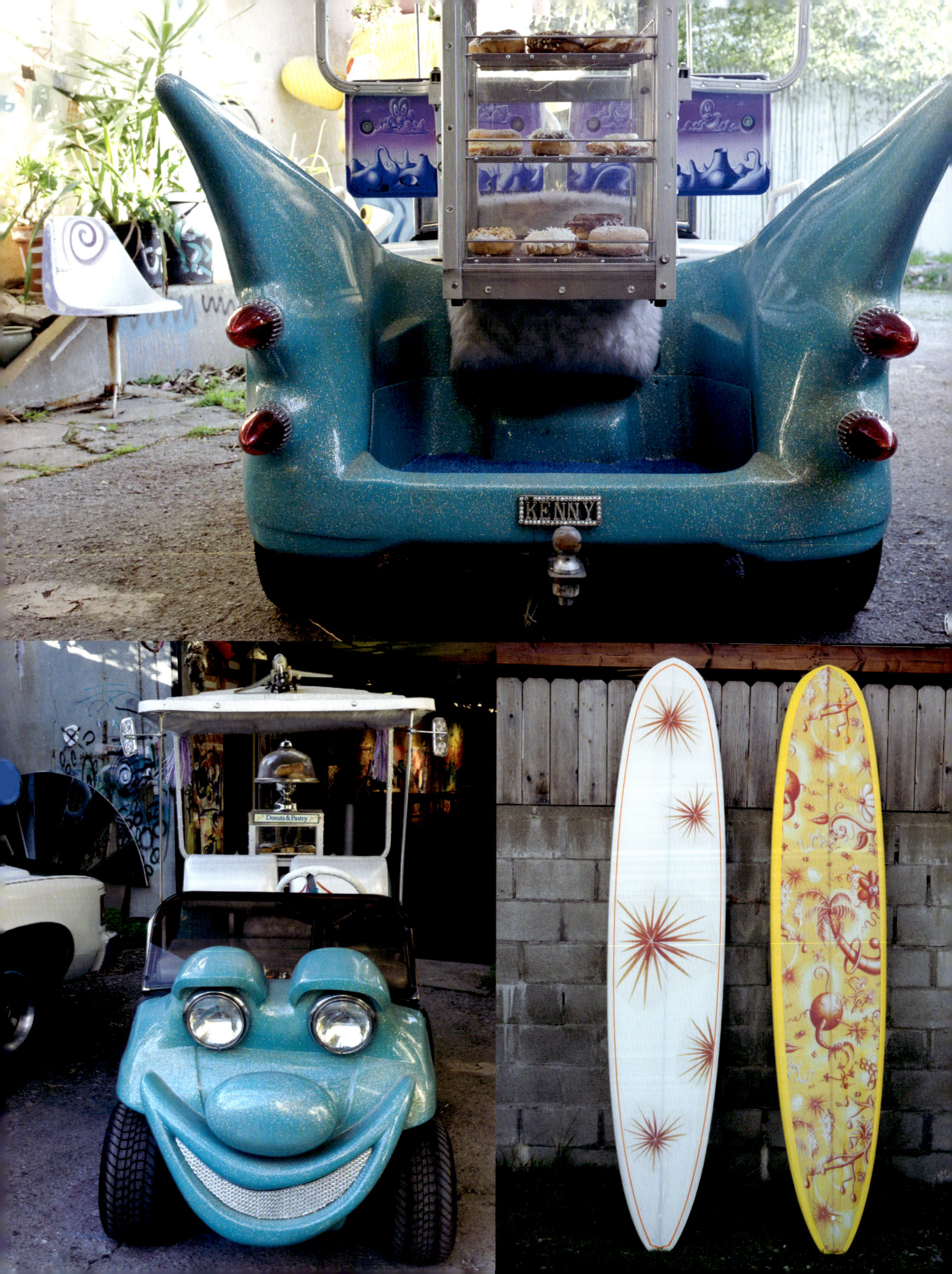
KENNY
Donuts & Pastry

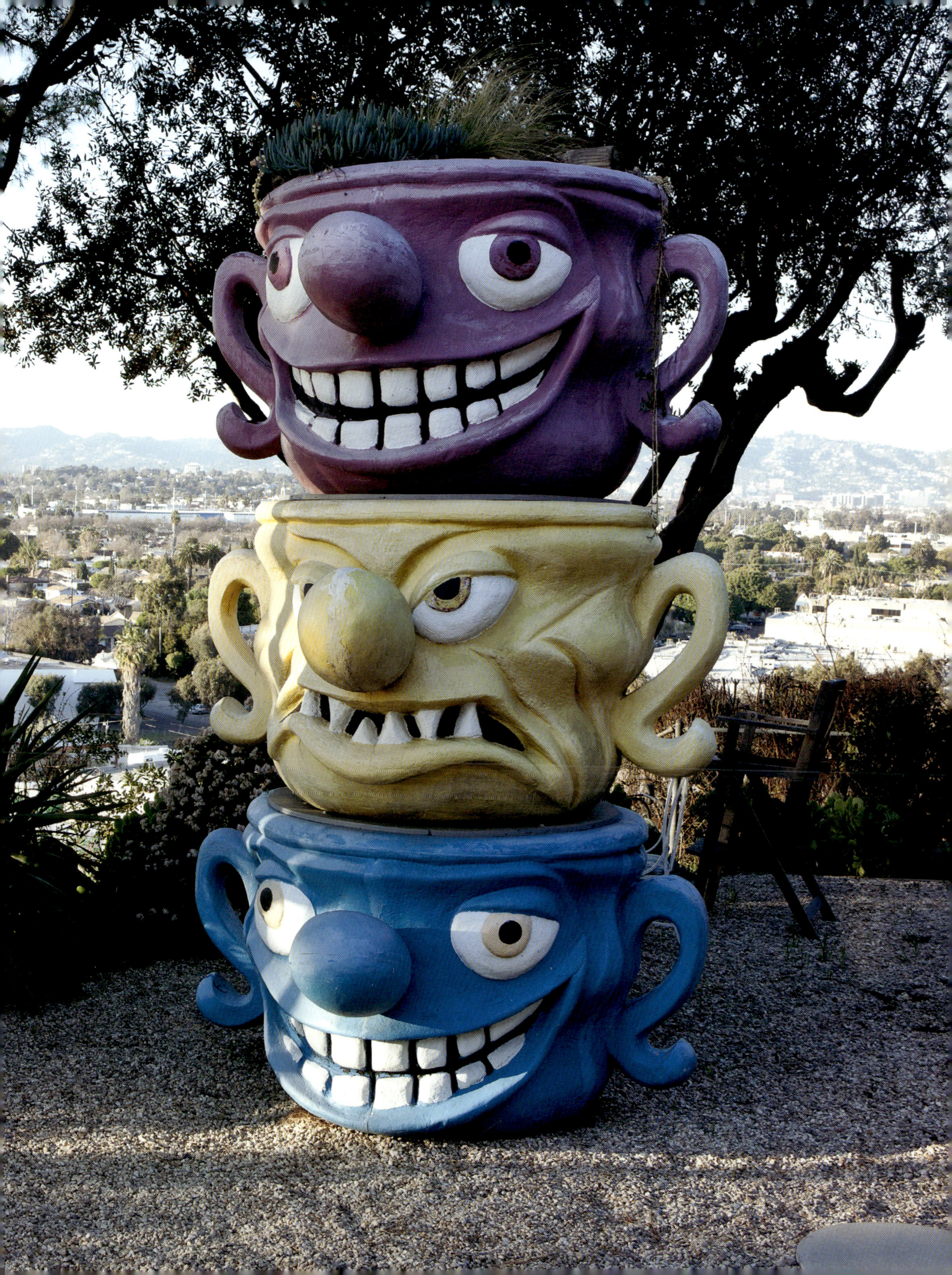

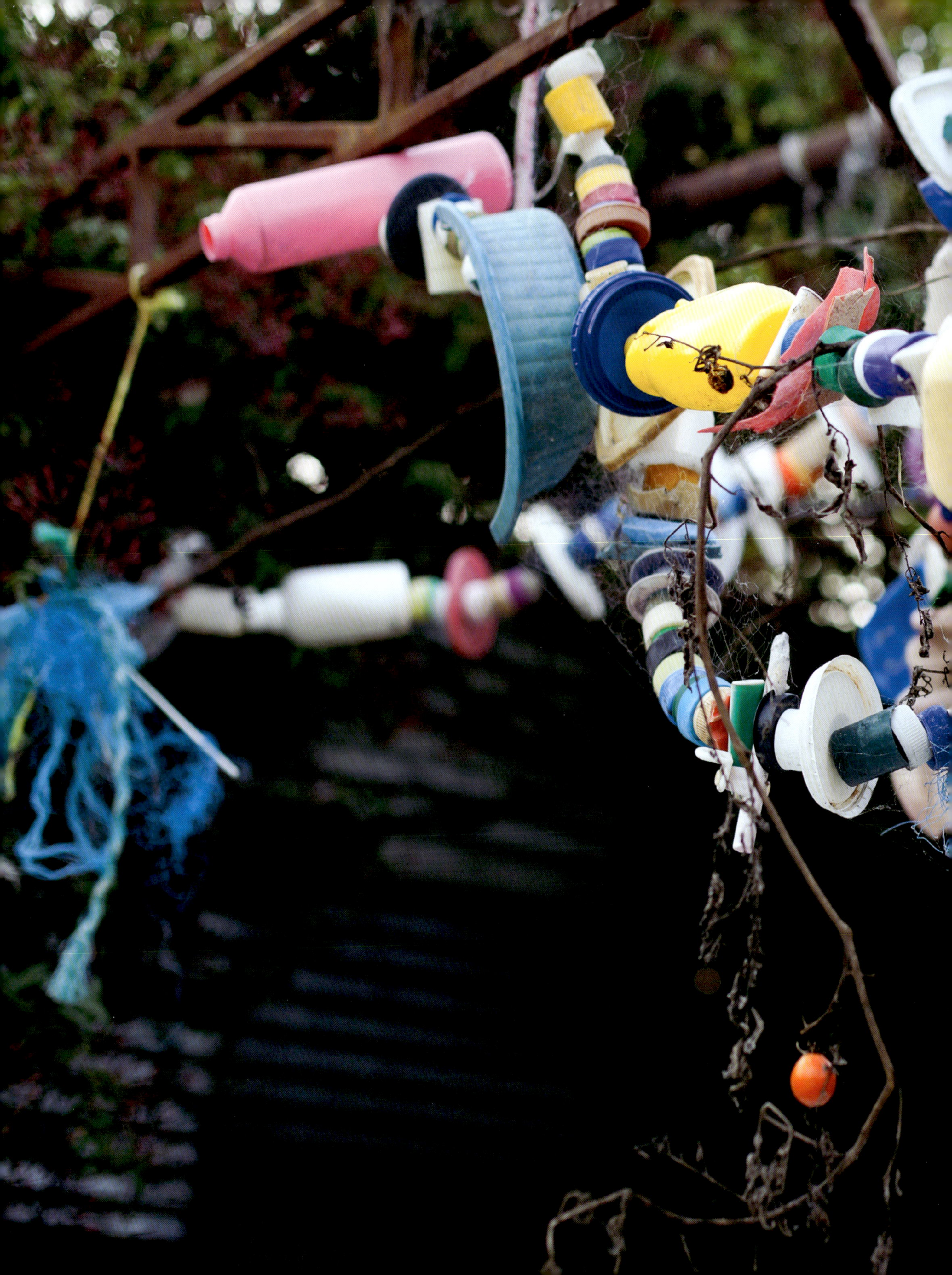

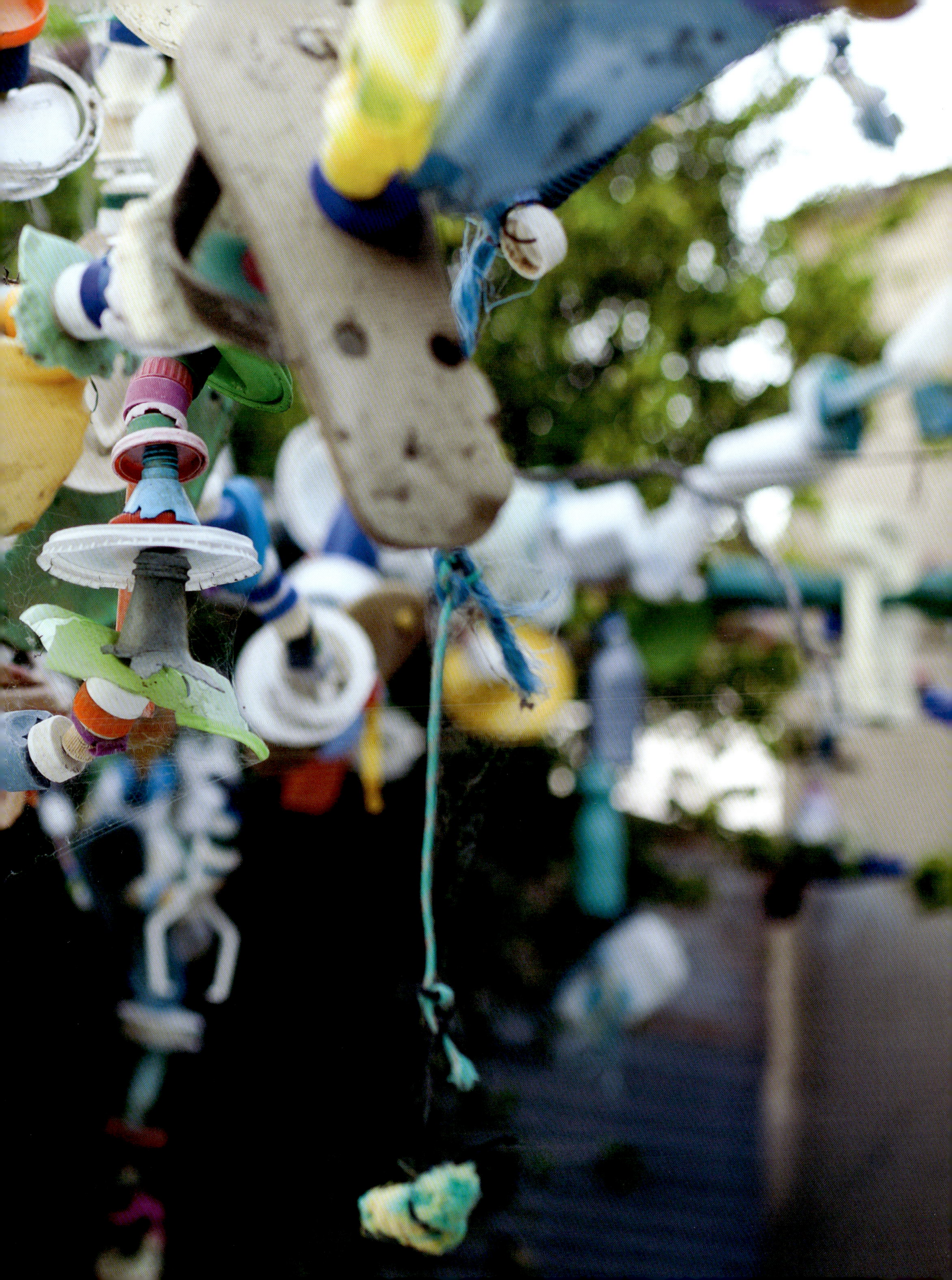

PAINTINGS & SCULPTURES

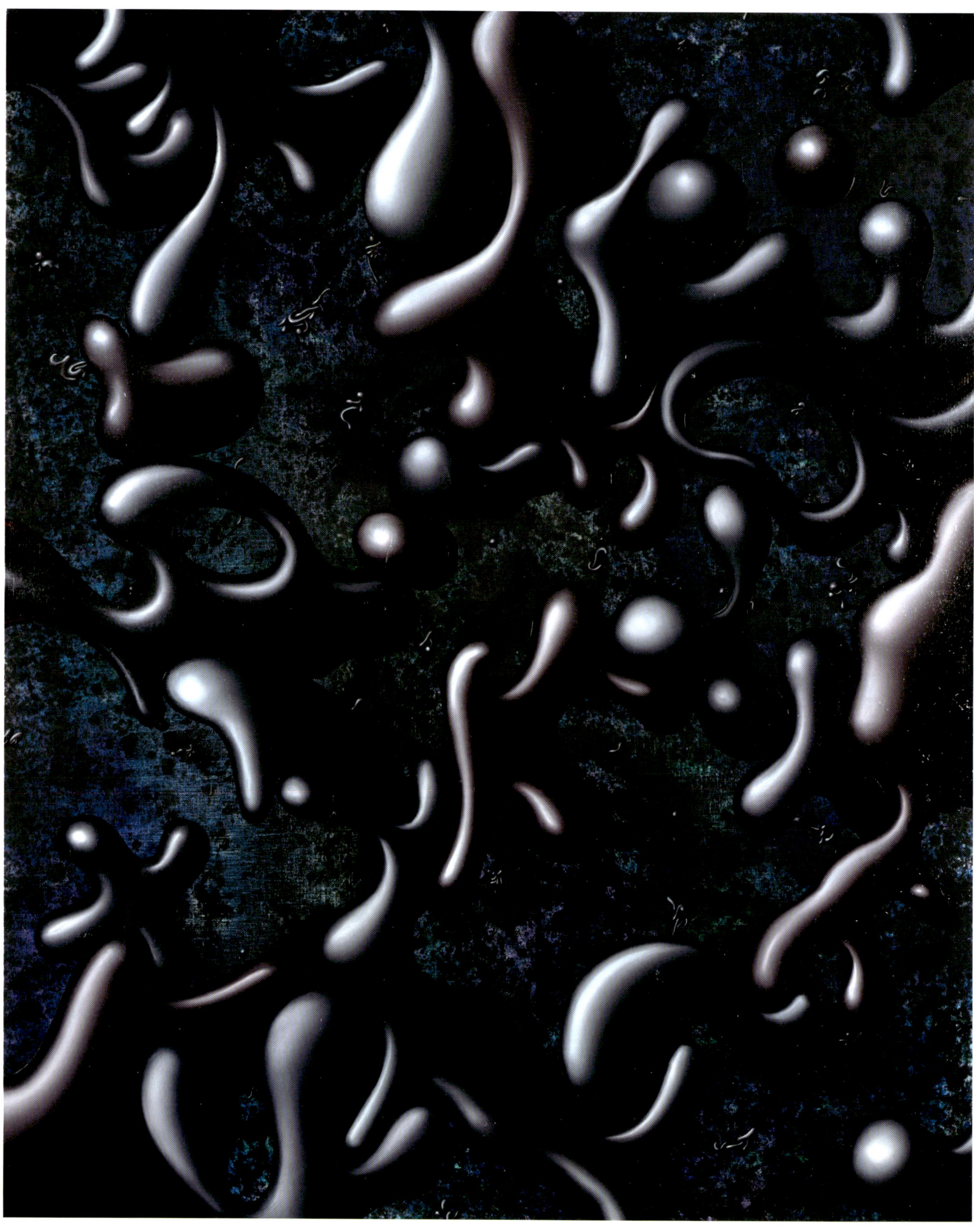

BLACK, 2012 - OIL & ACRYLIC ON LINEN / 72 X 60 INCHES

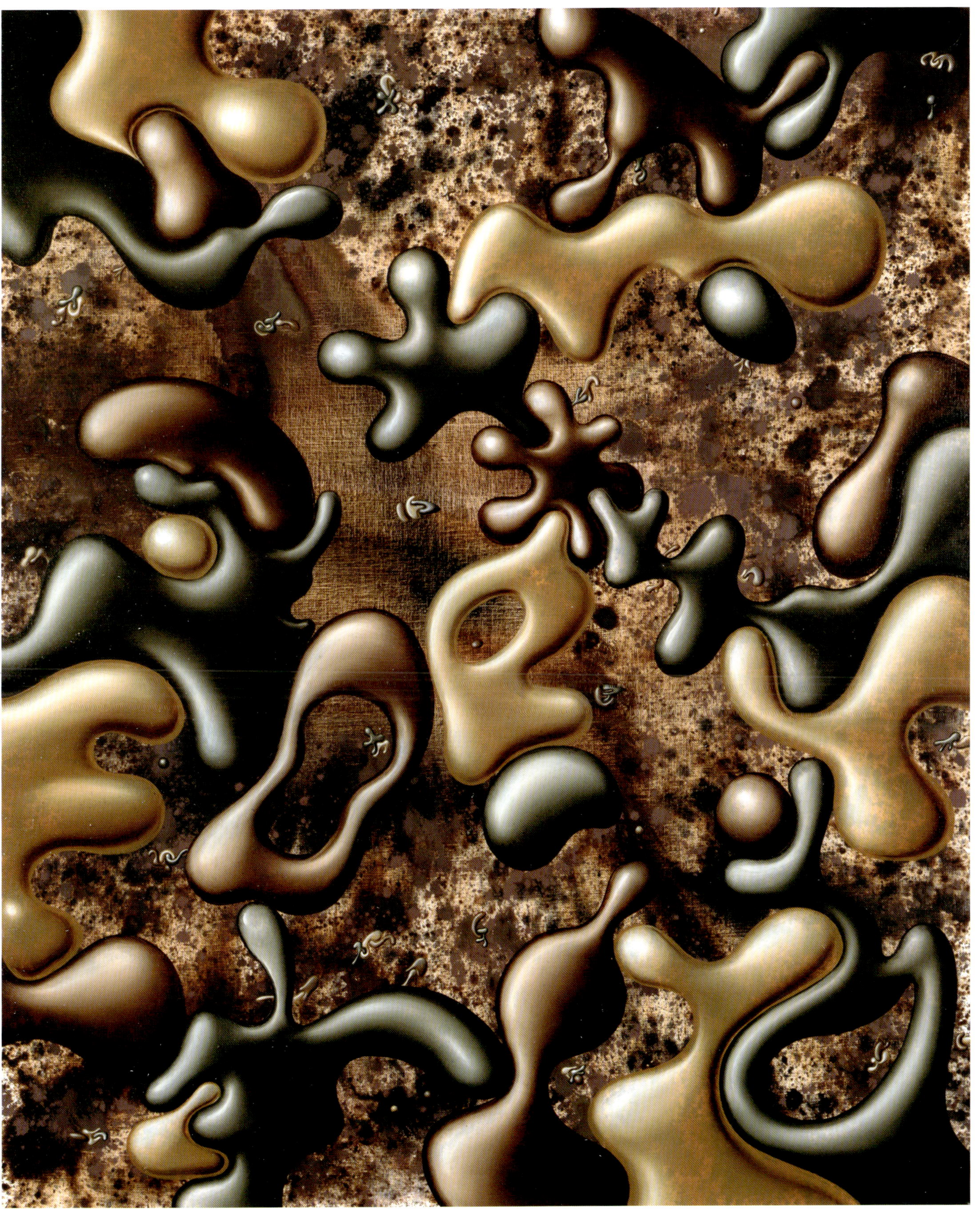

BROWN, 2012 - OIL & ACRYLIC ON LINEN / 72 X 60 INCHES

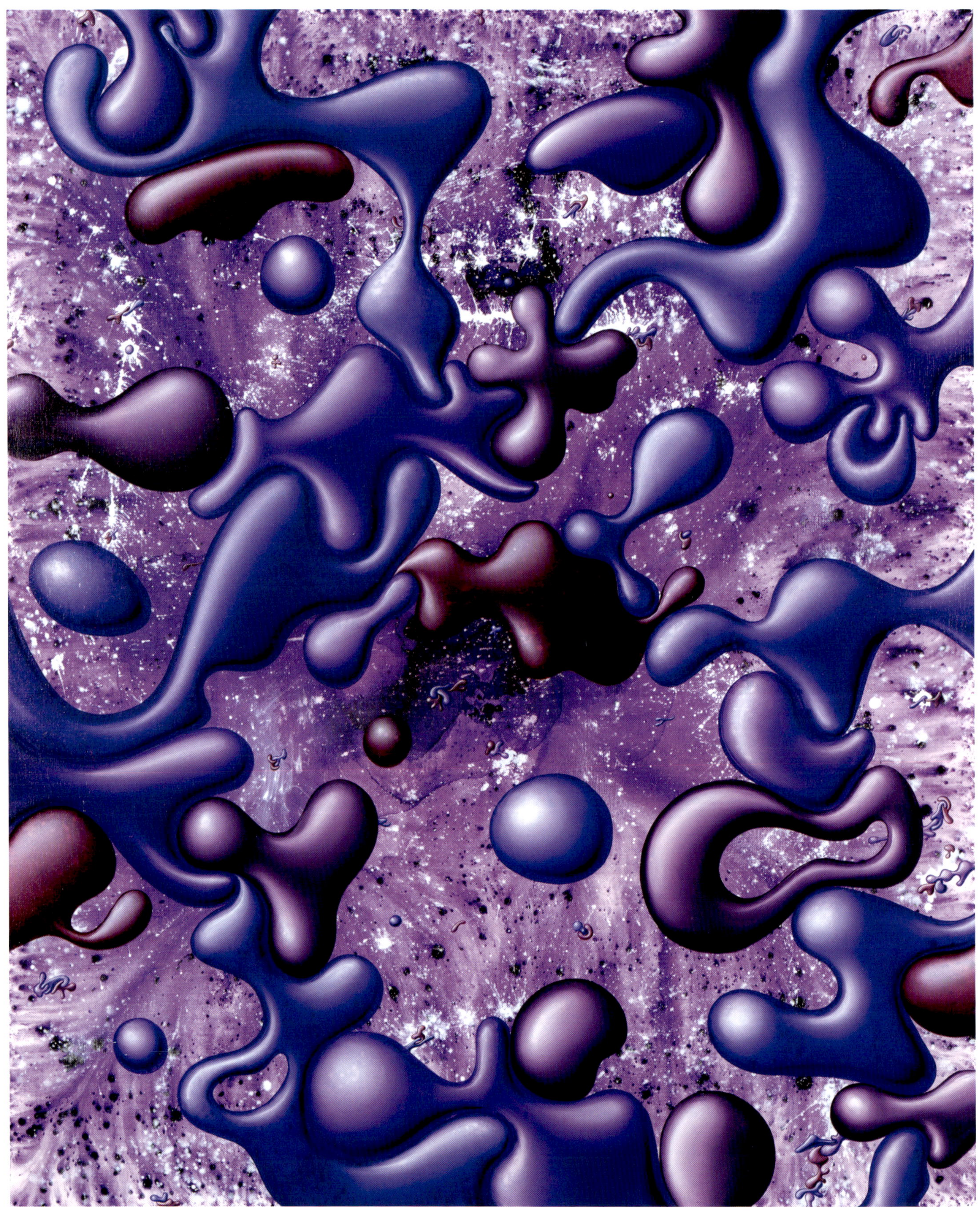

PURPLE, 2012 - OIL & ACRYLIC ON LINEN / 72 X 60 INCHES

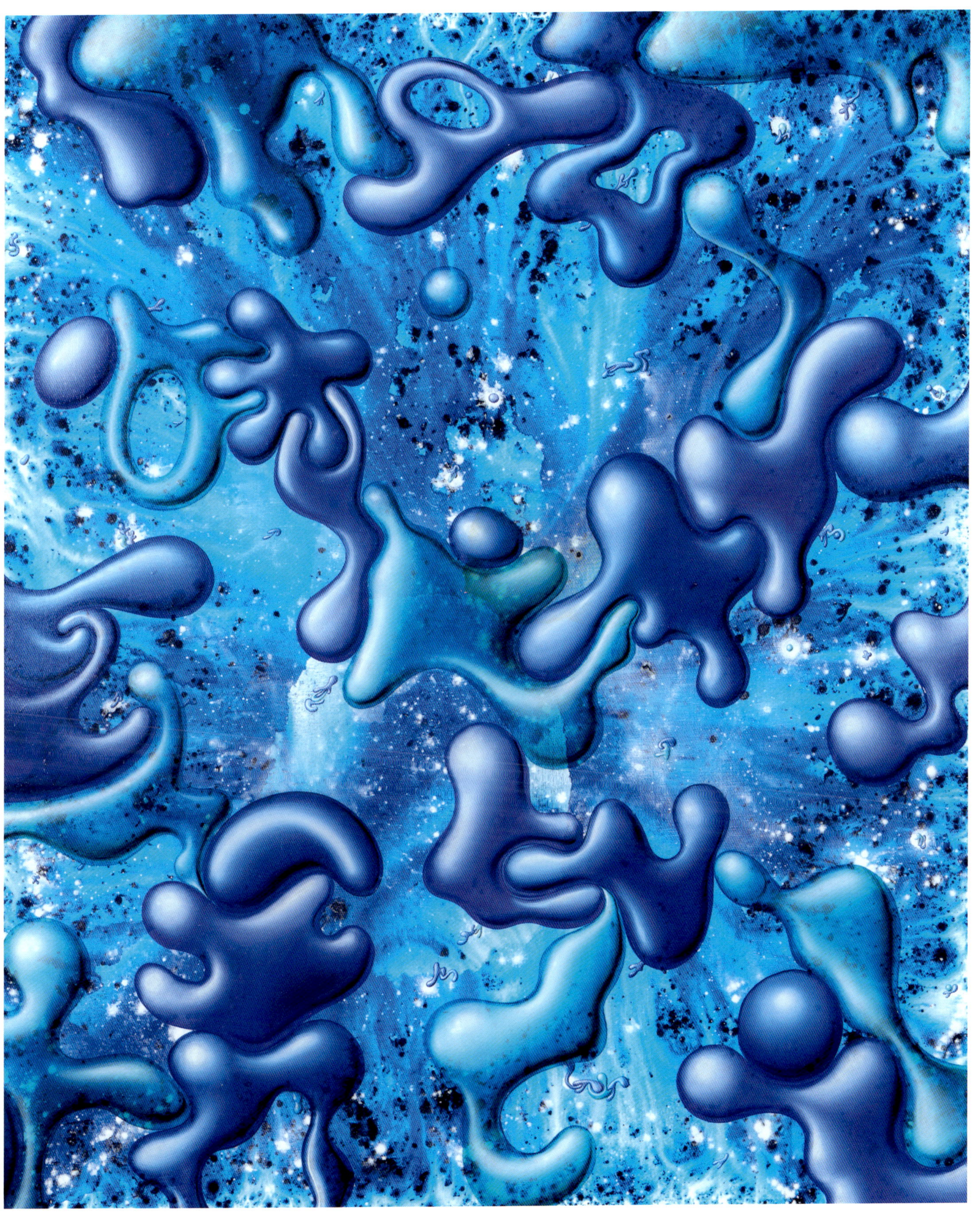

BLUE, 2012 - OIL & ACRYLIC ON LINEN / 72 X 60 INCHES

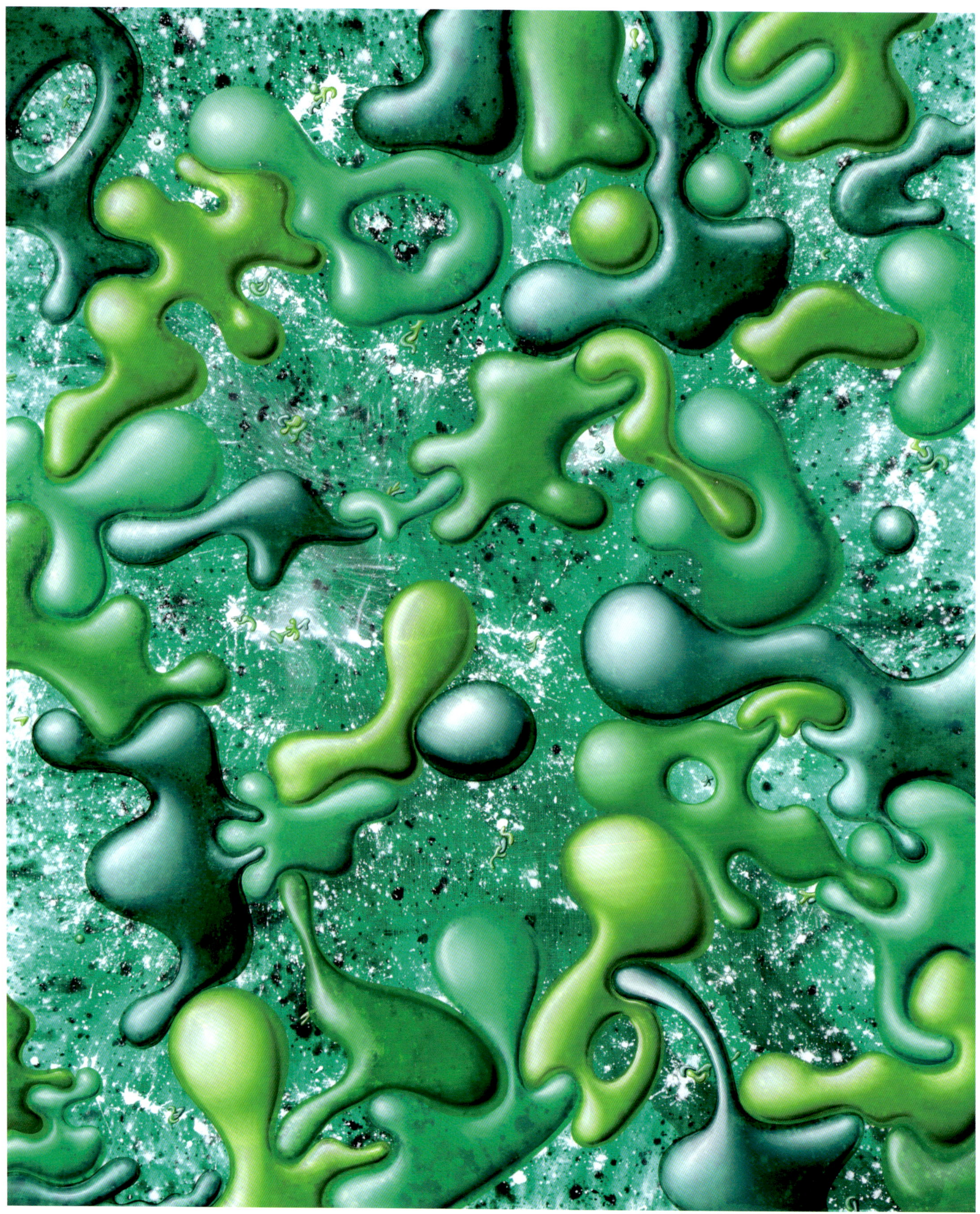

GREEN, 2012 - OIL & ACRYLIC ON LINEN / 72 X 60 INCHES

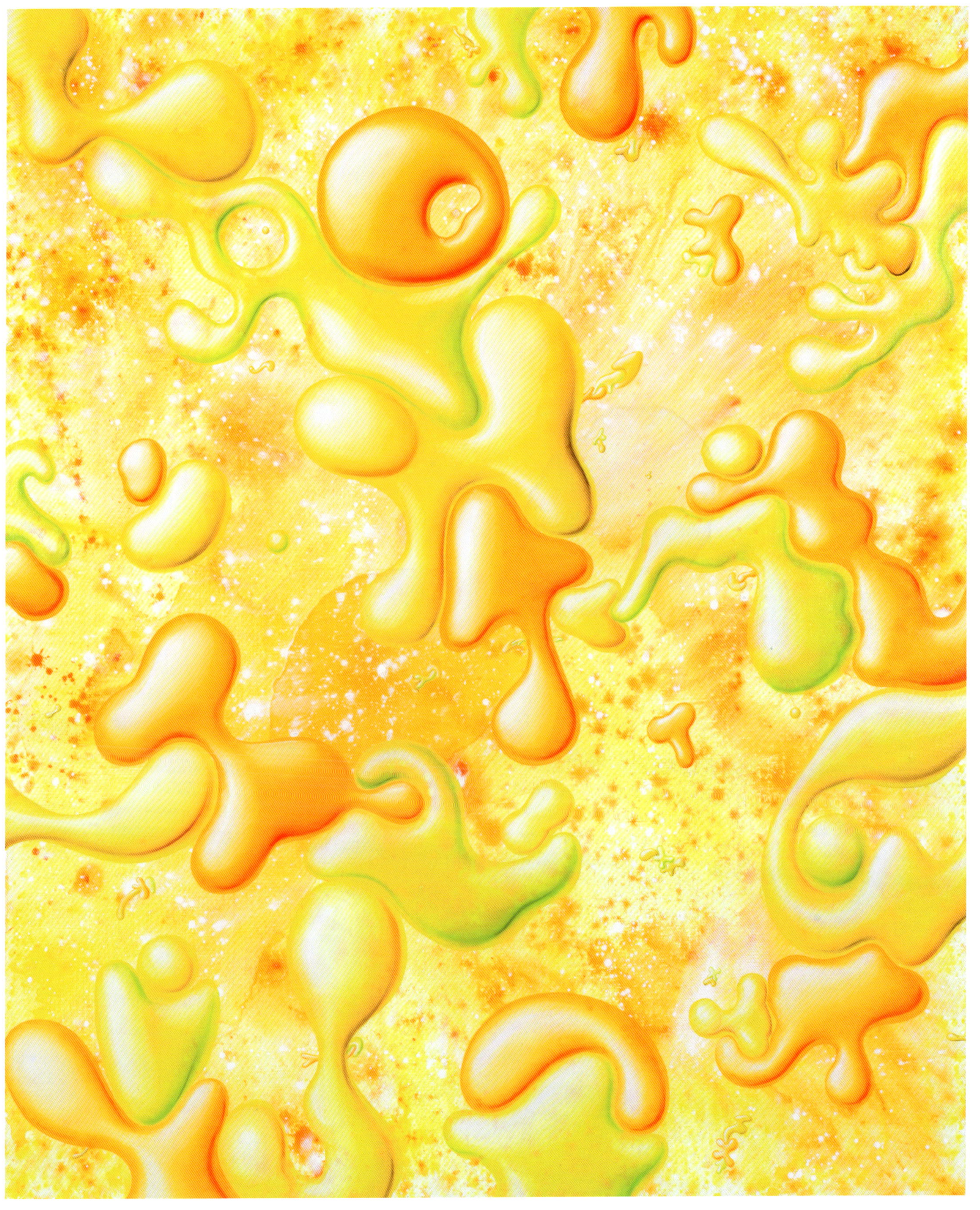

YELLOW, 2012 - OIL & ACRYLIC ON LINEN / 72 X 60 INCHES

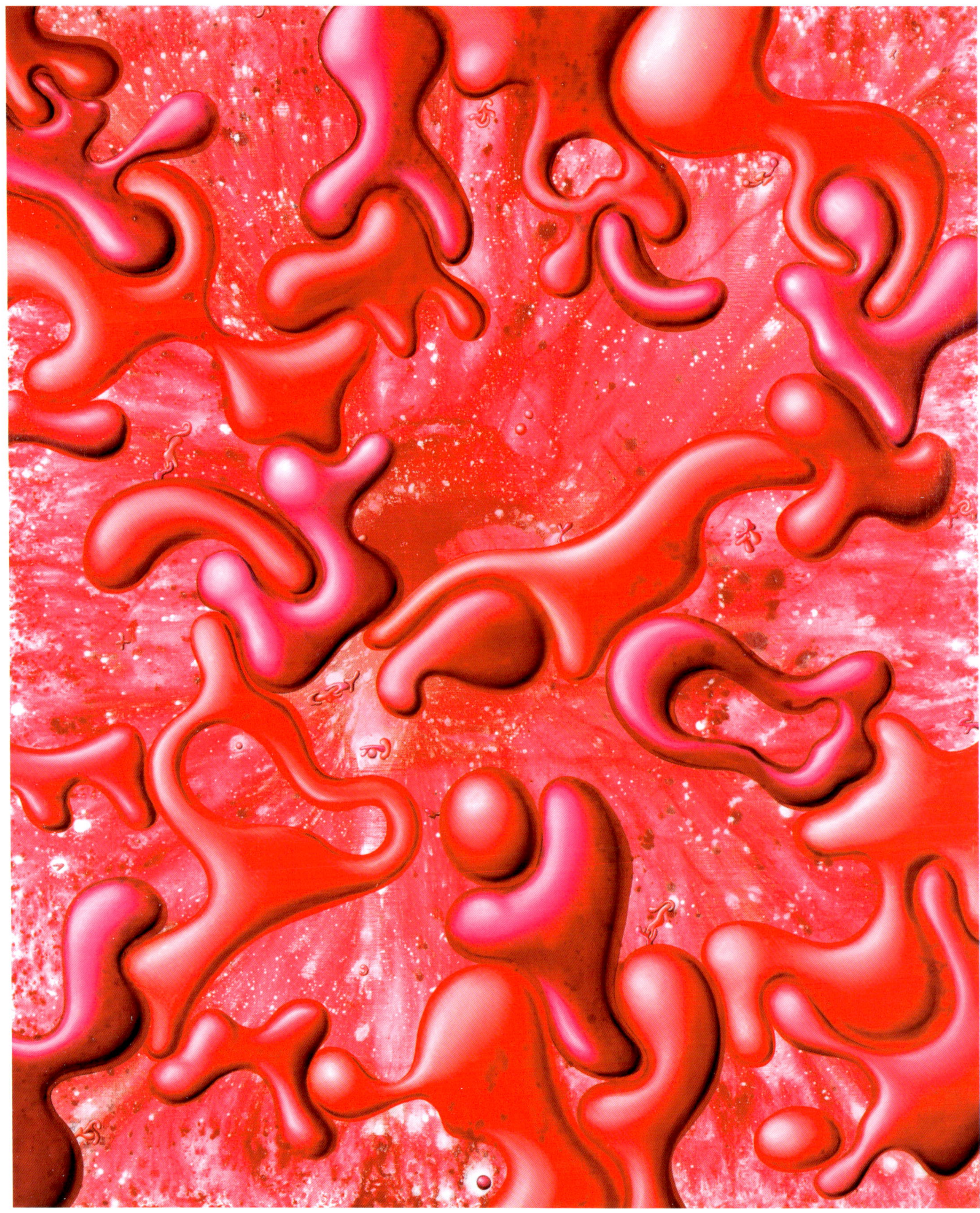

RED, 2012 - OIL & ACRYLIC ON LINEN / 72 X 60 INCHES

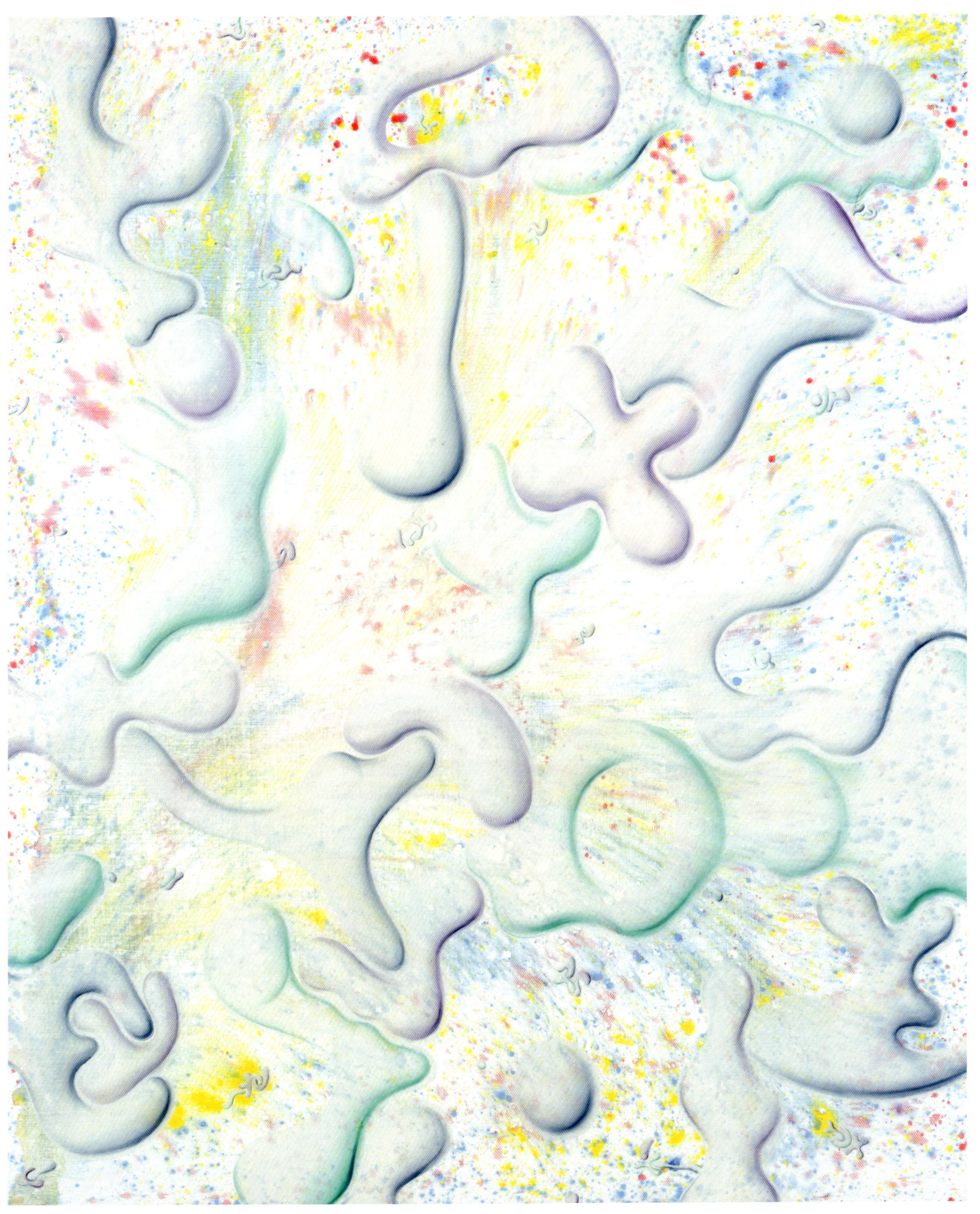

WHITE, 2012 - OIL & ACRYLIC ON LINEN / 72 X 60 INCHES

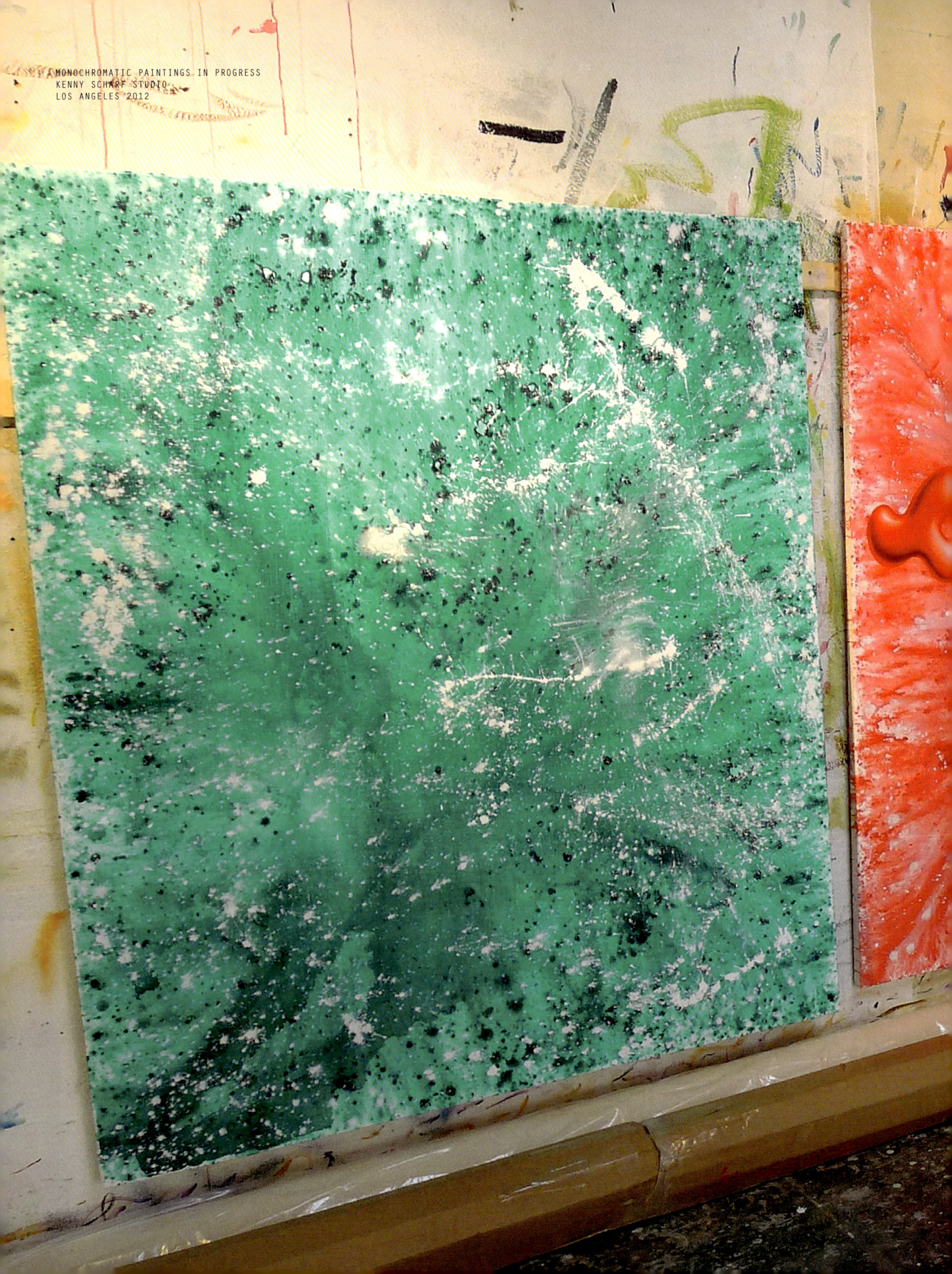

MONOCHROMATIC PAINTINGS IN PROGRESS
KENNY SCHARF STUDIO
LOS ANGELES 2012

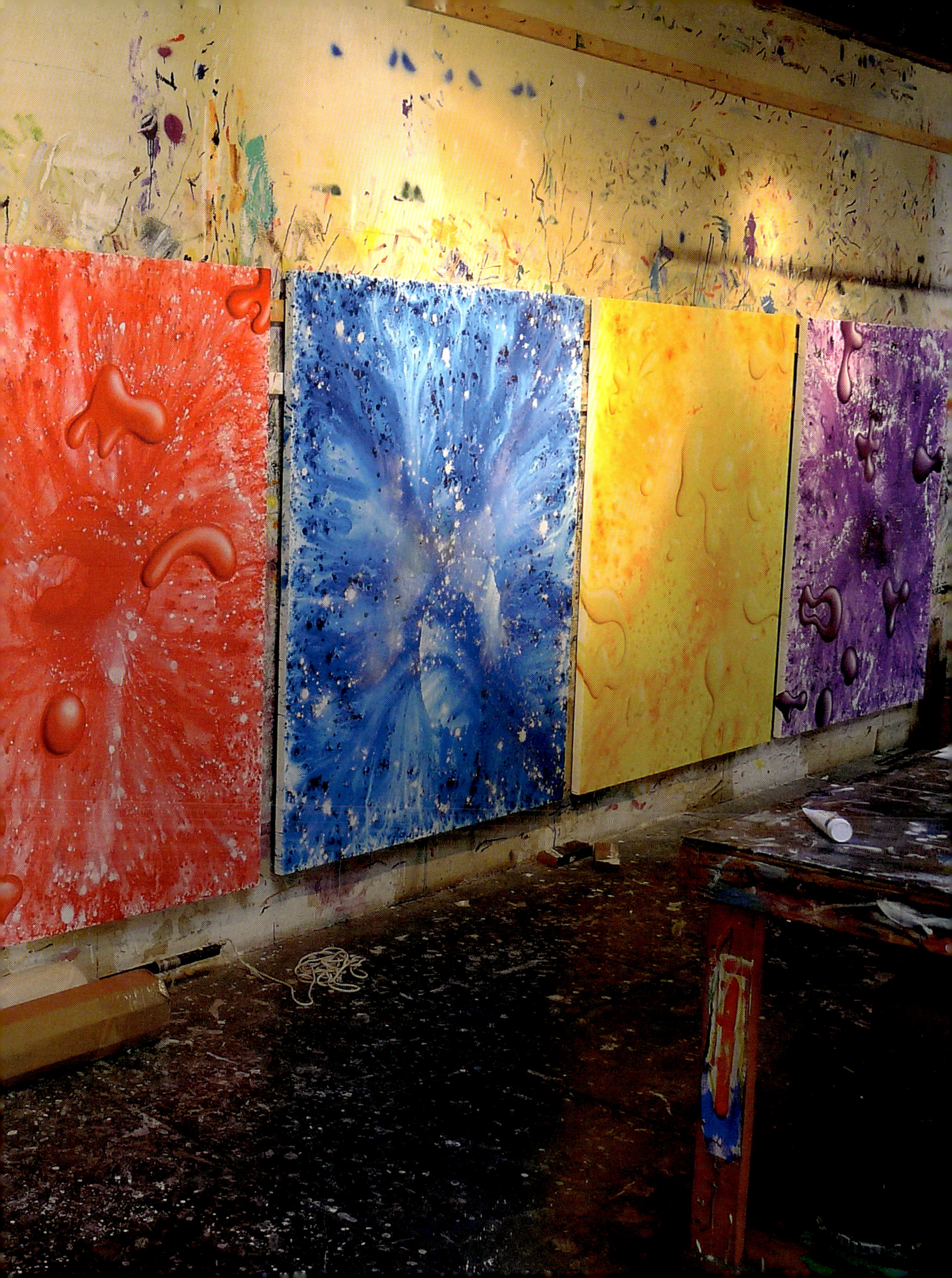

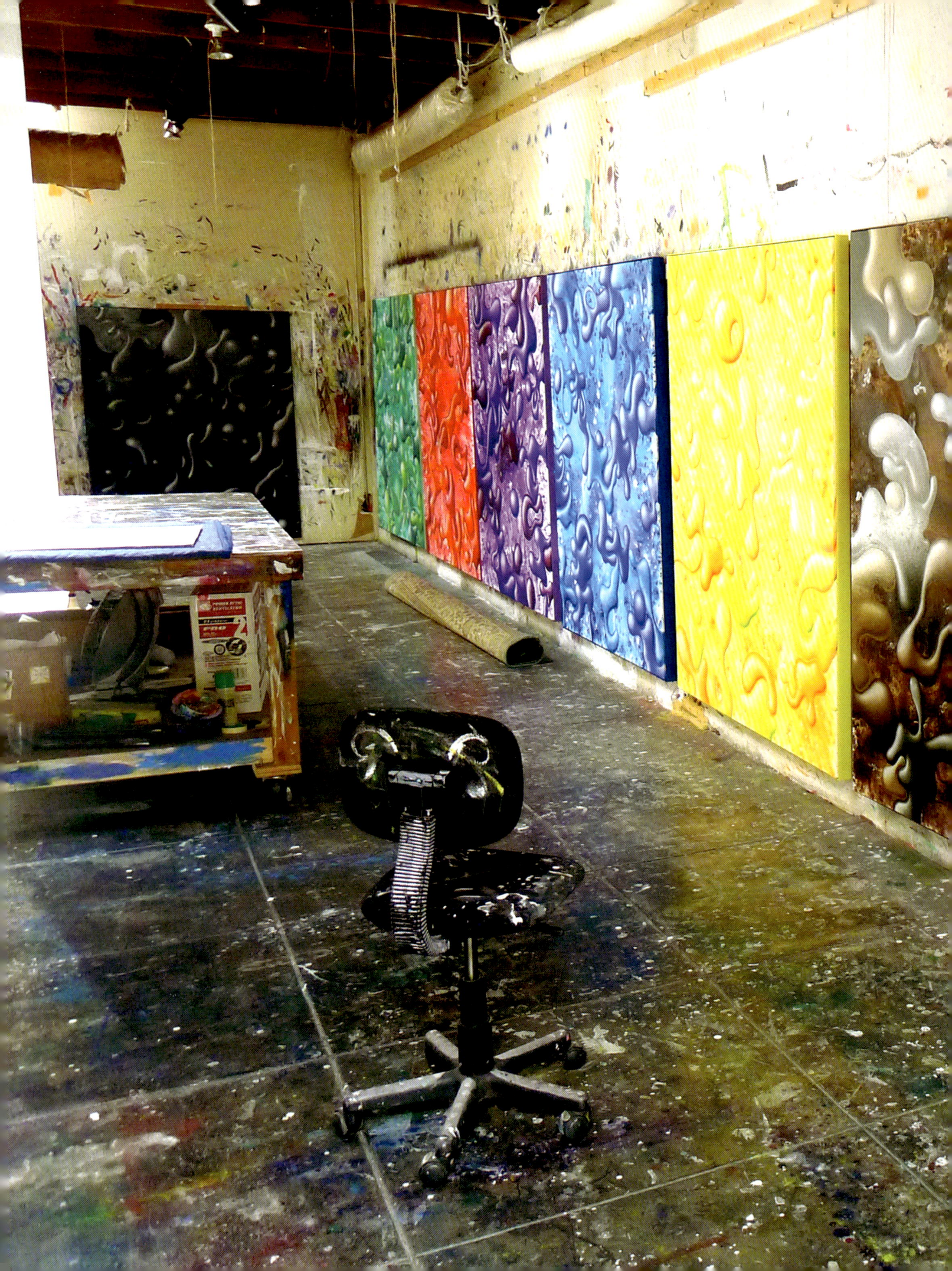

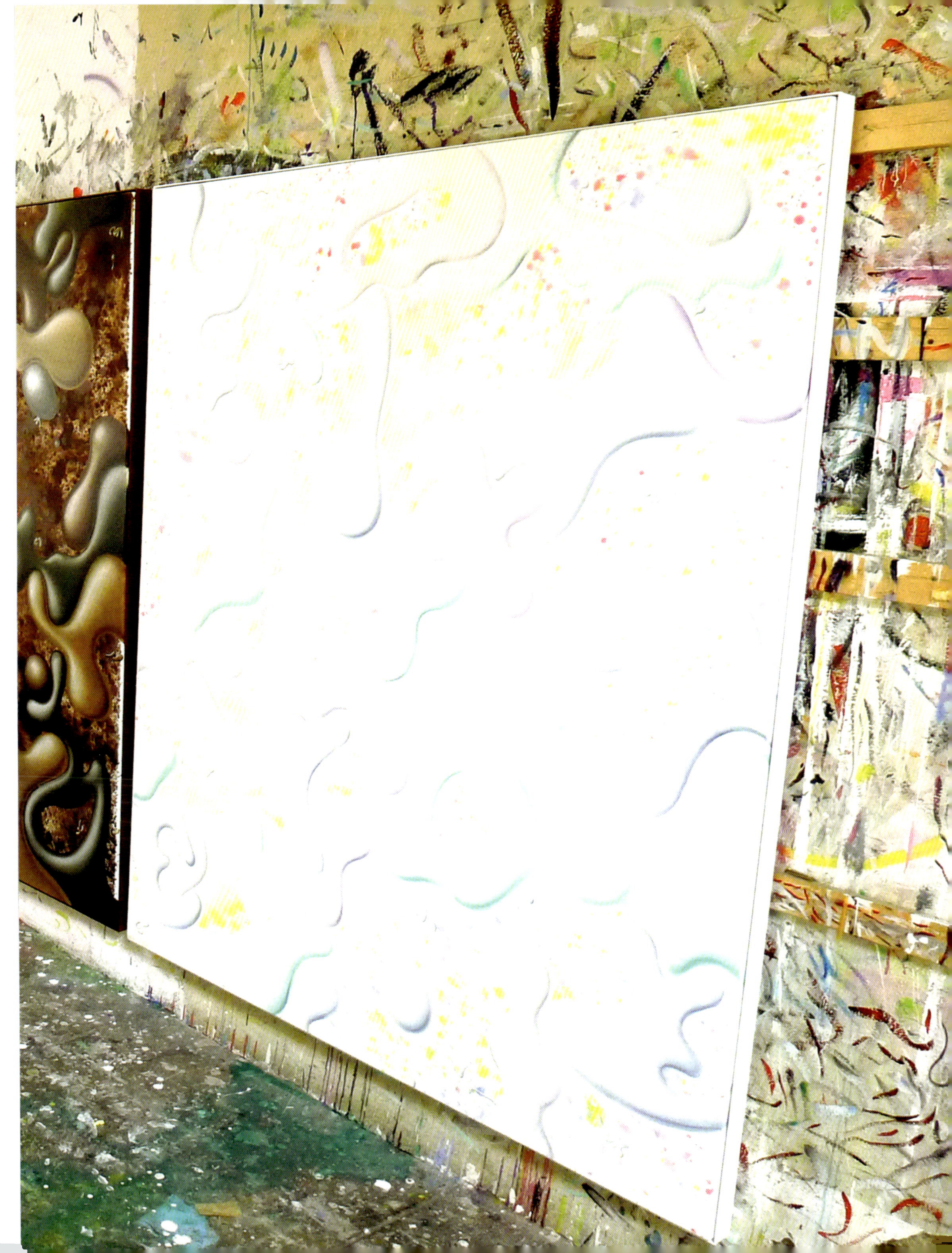

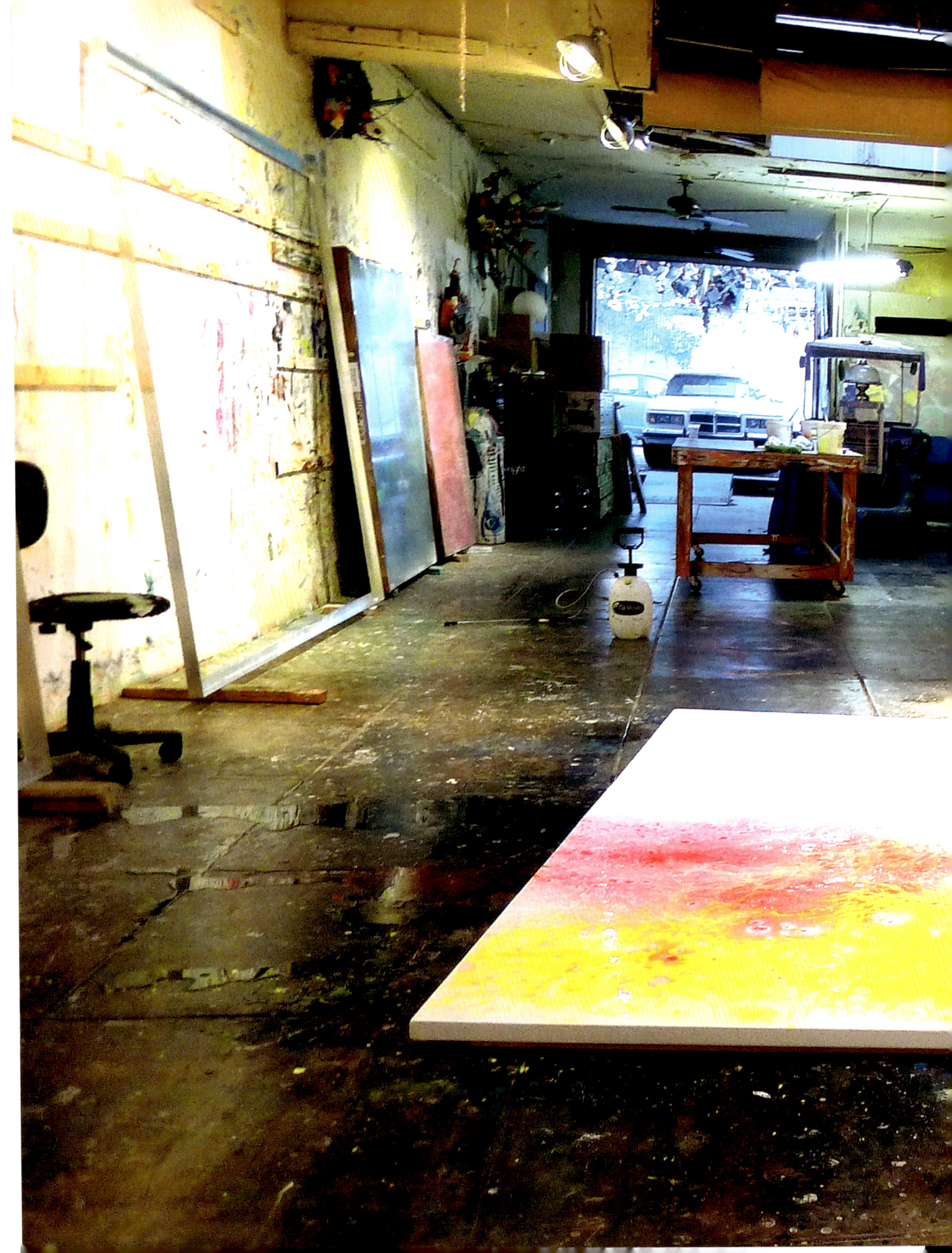

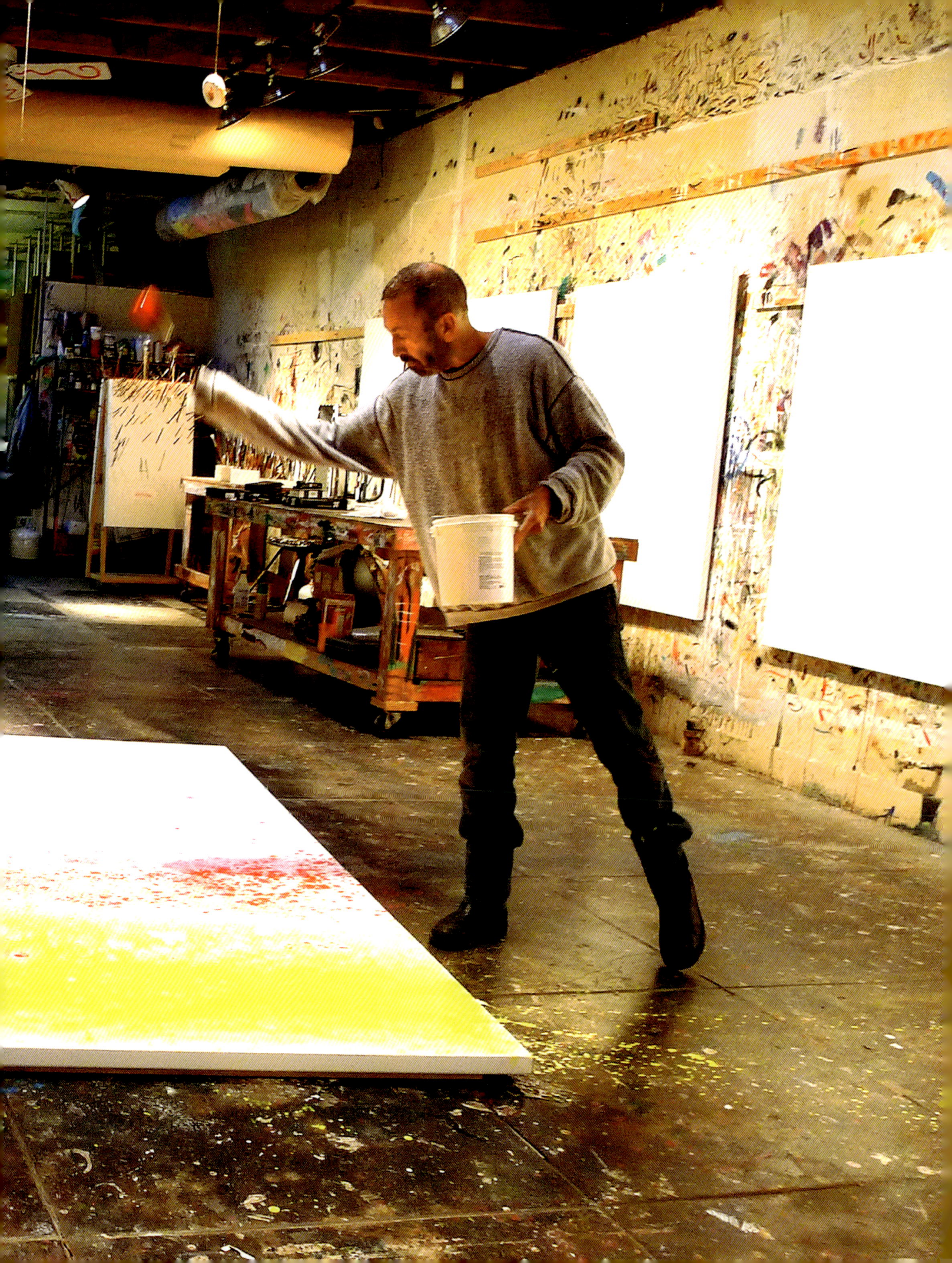

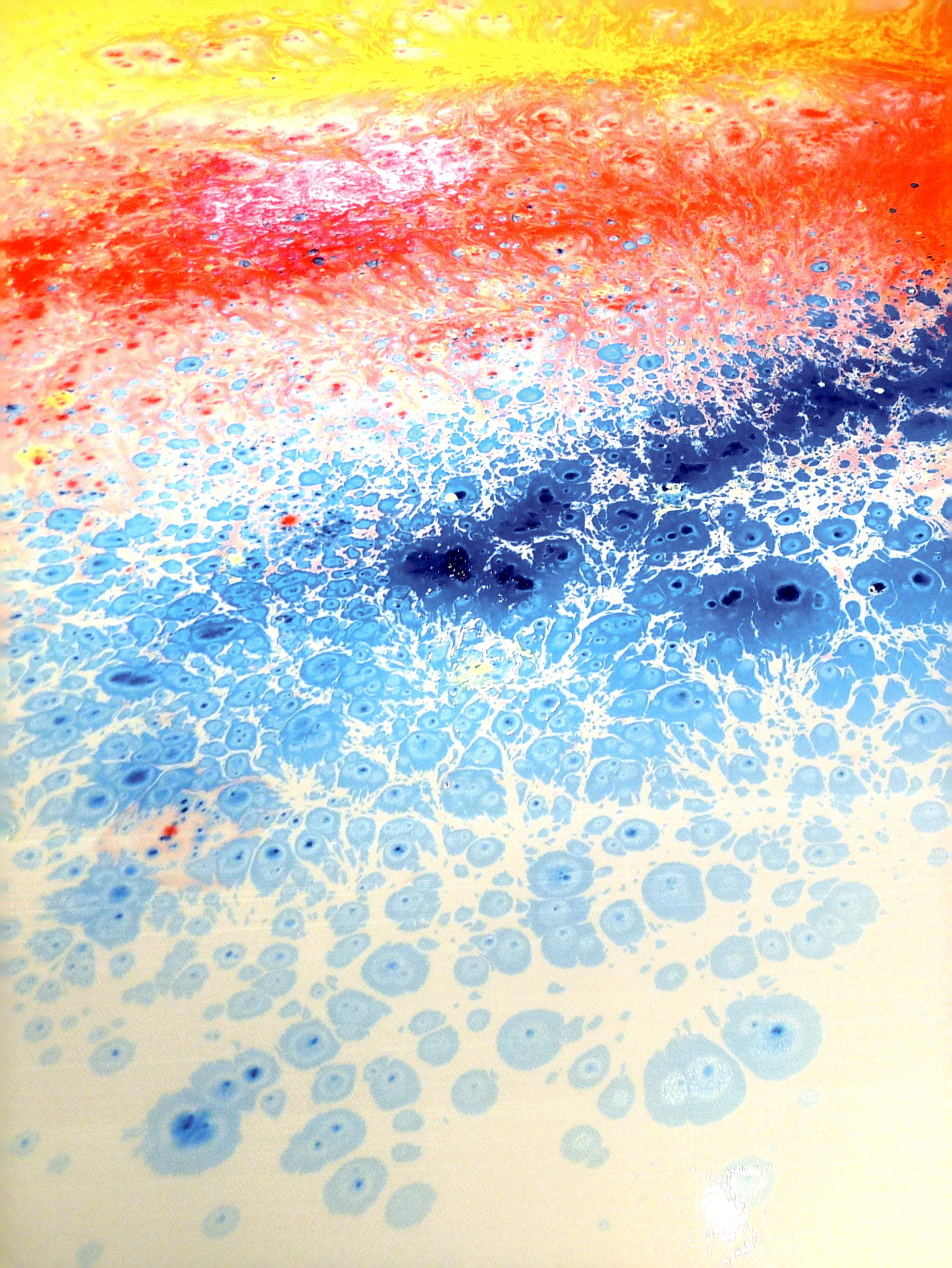

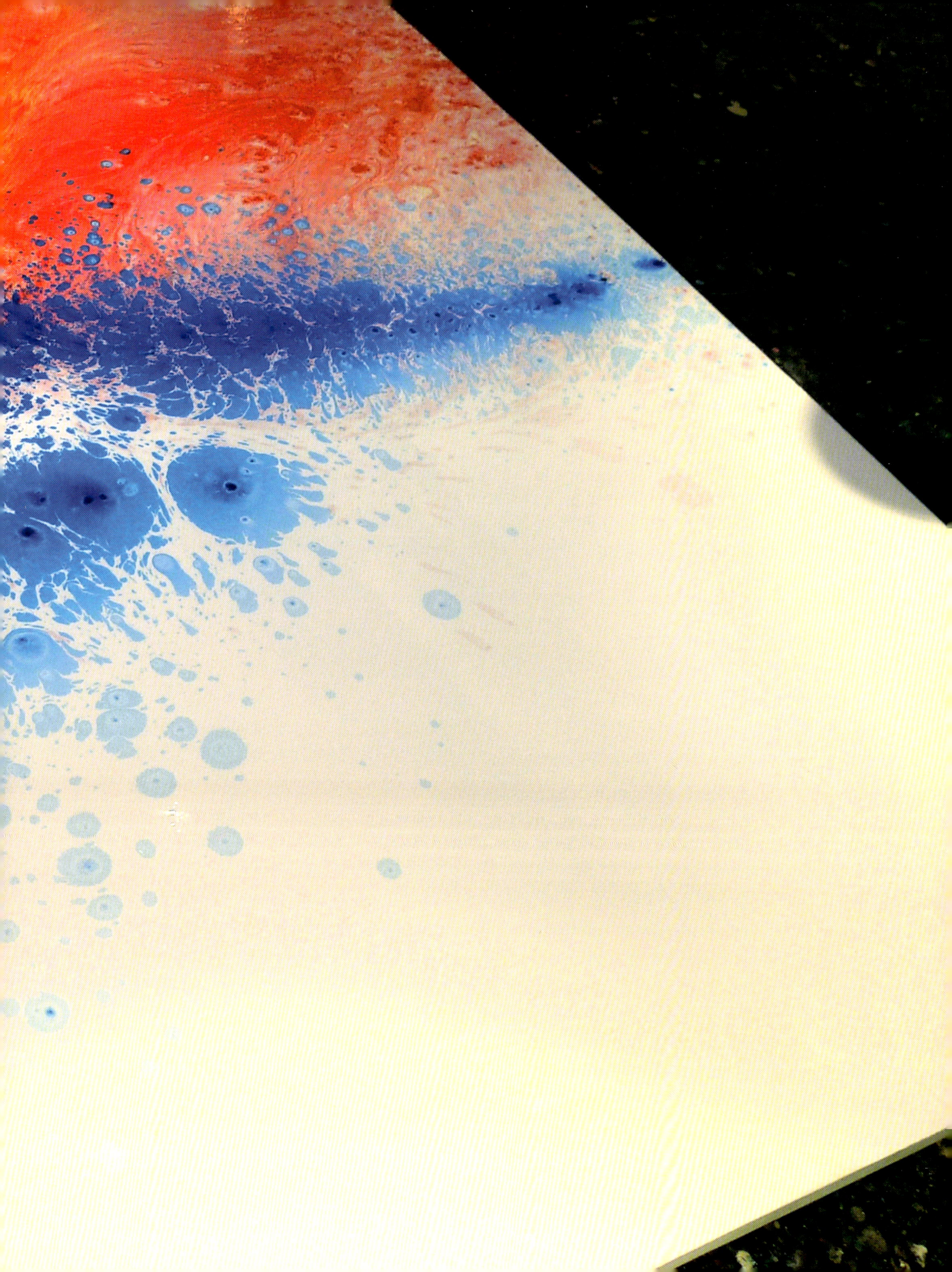

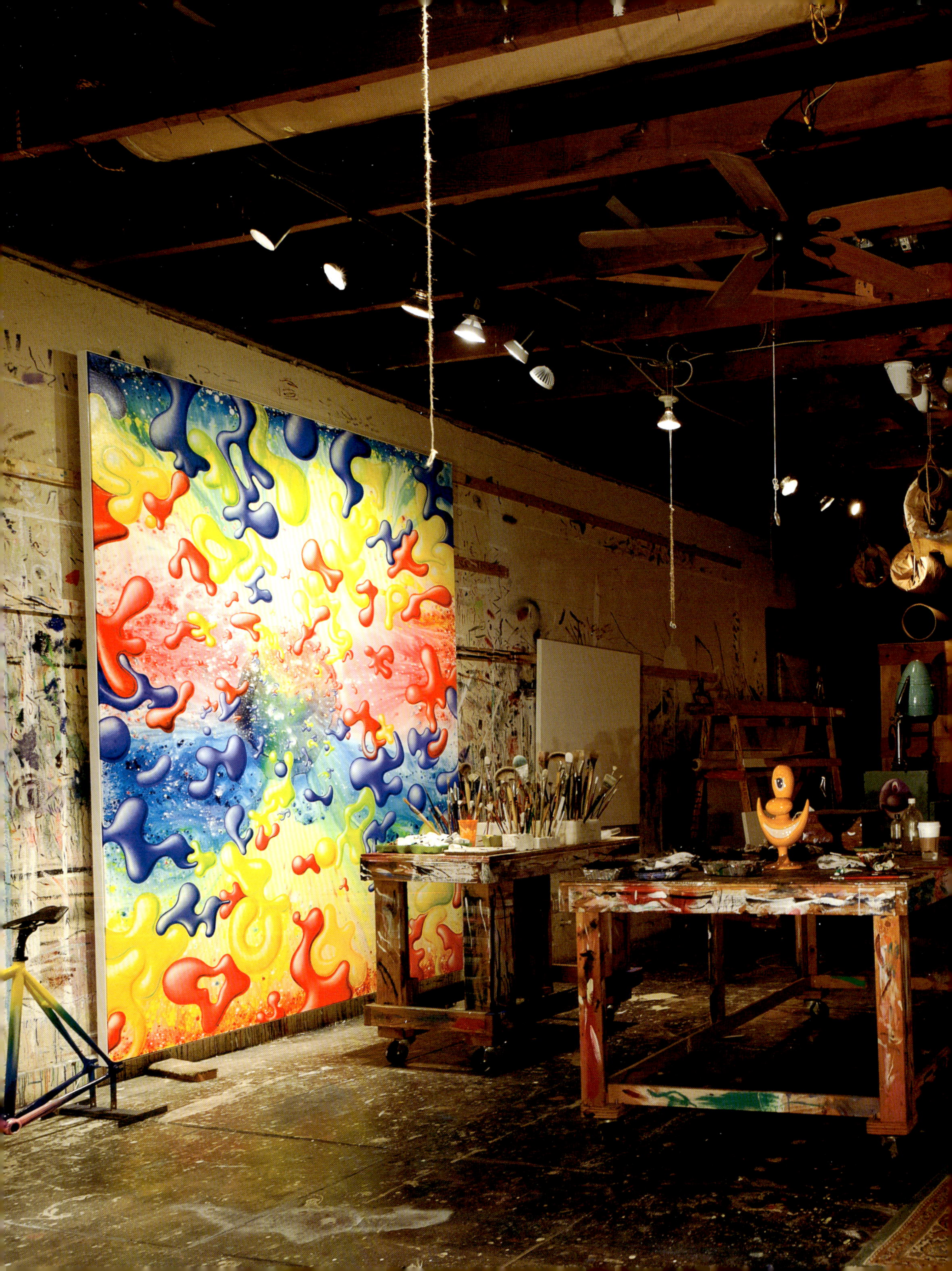

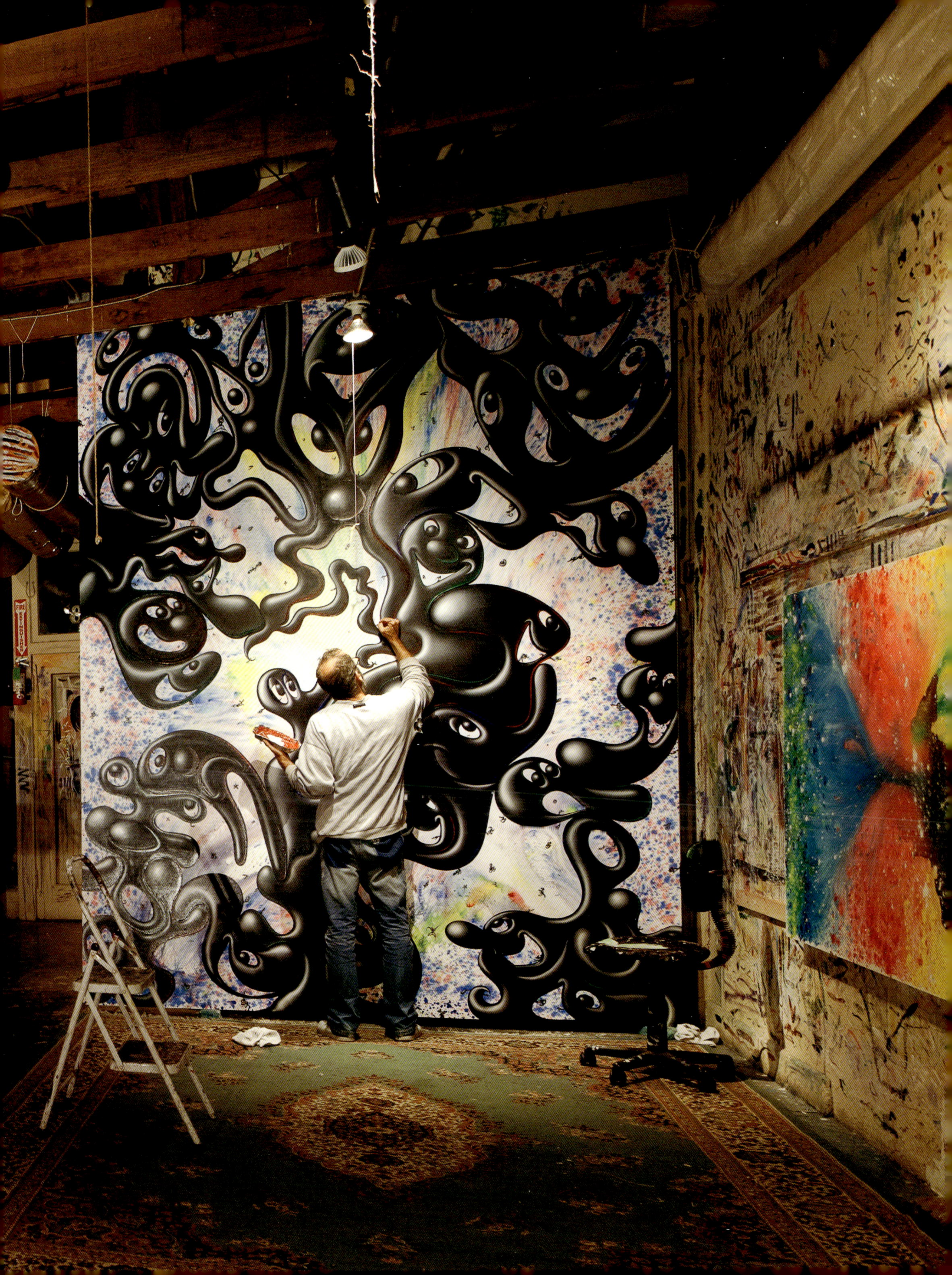

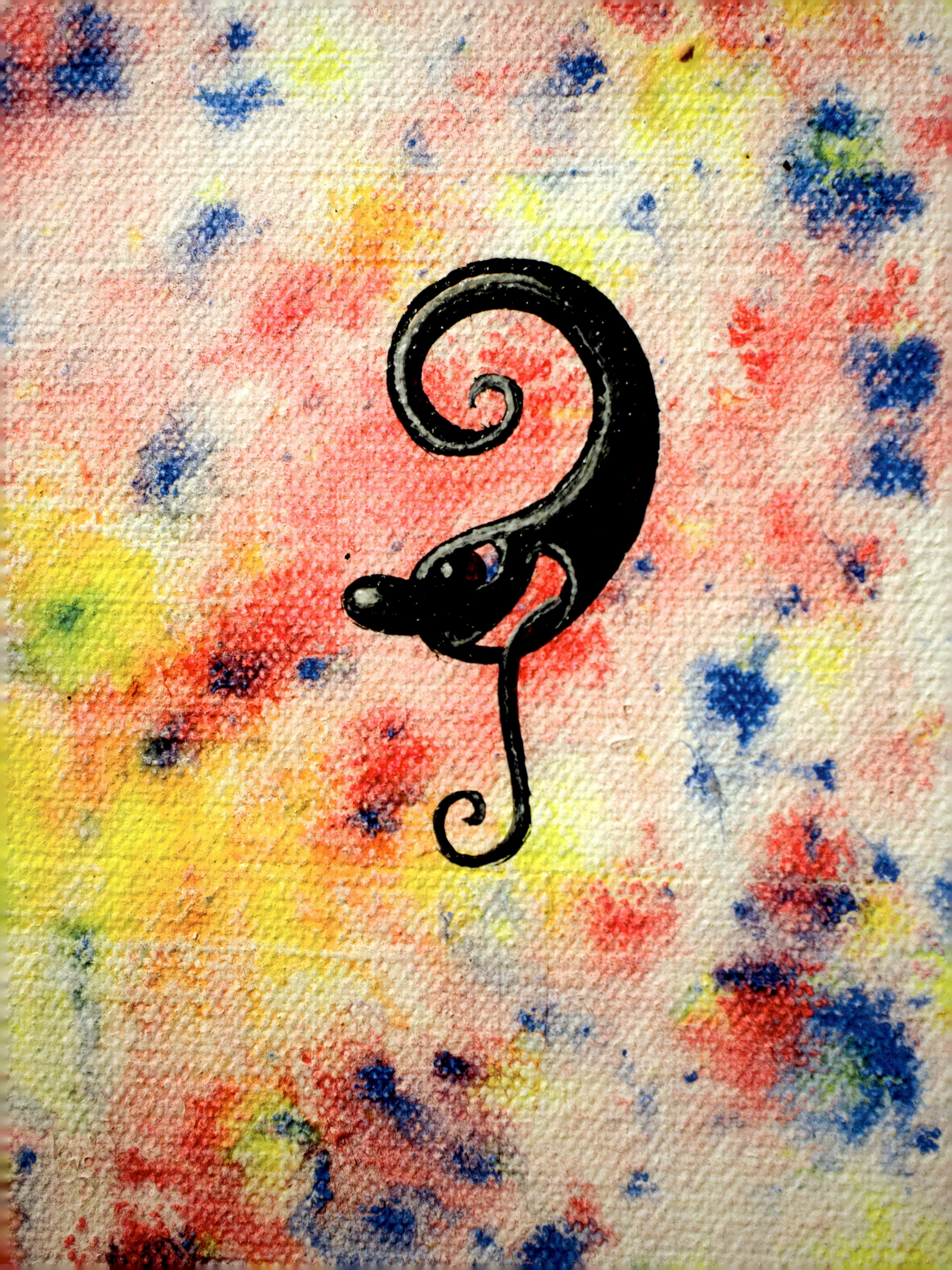

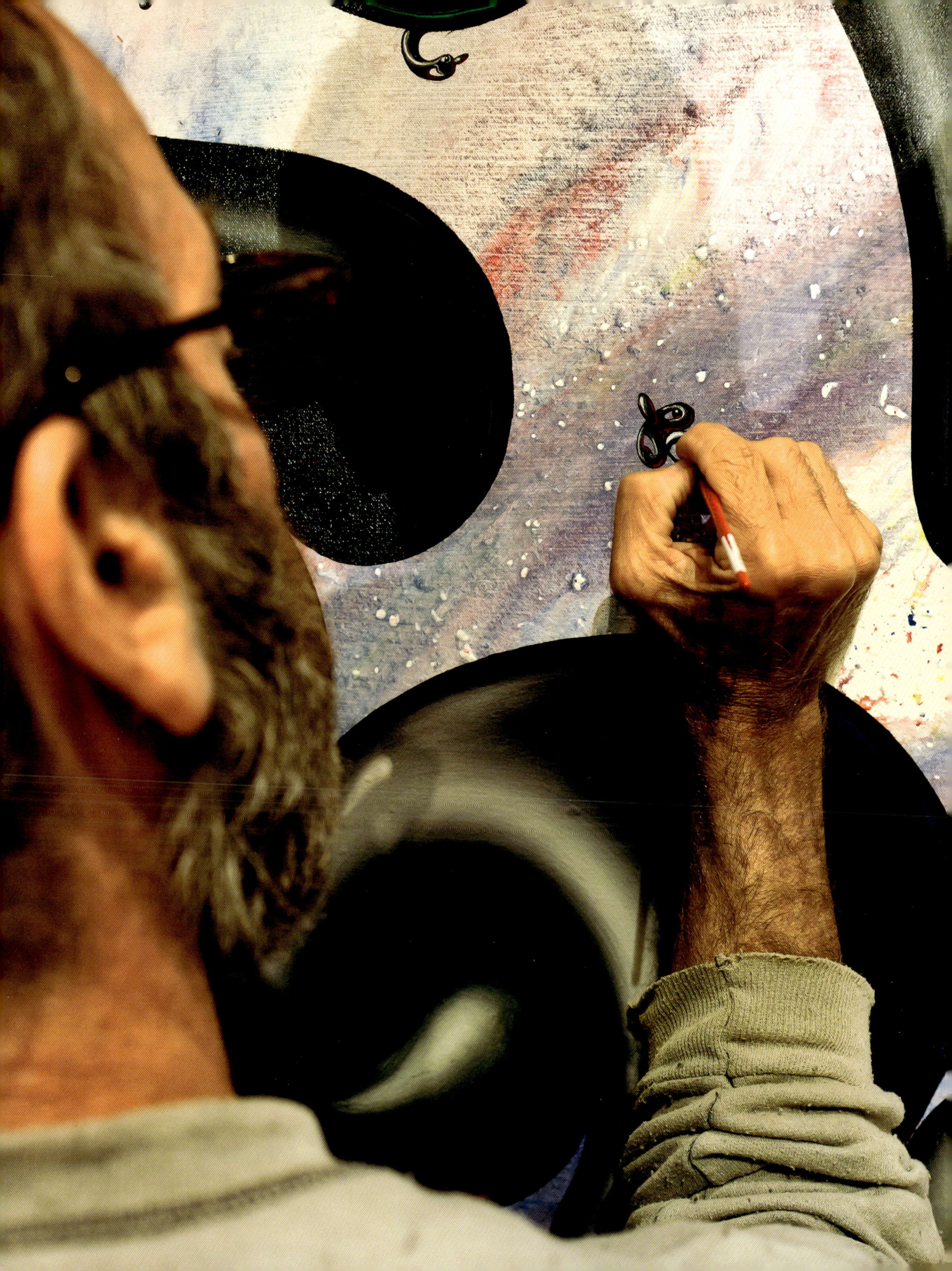

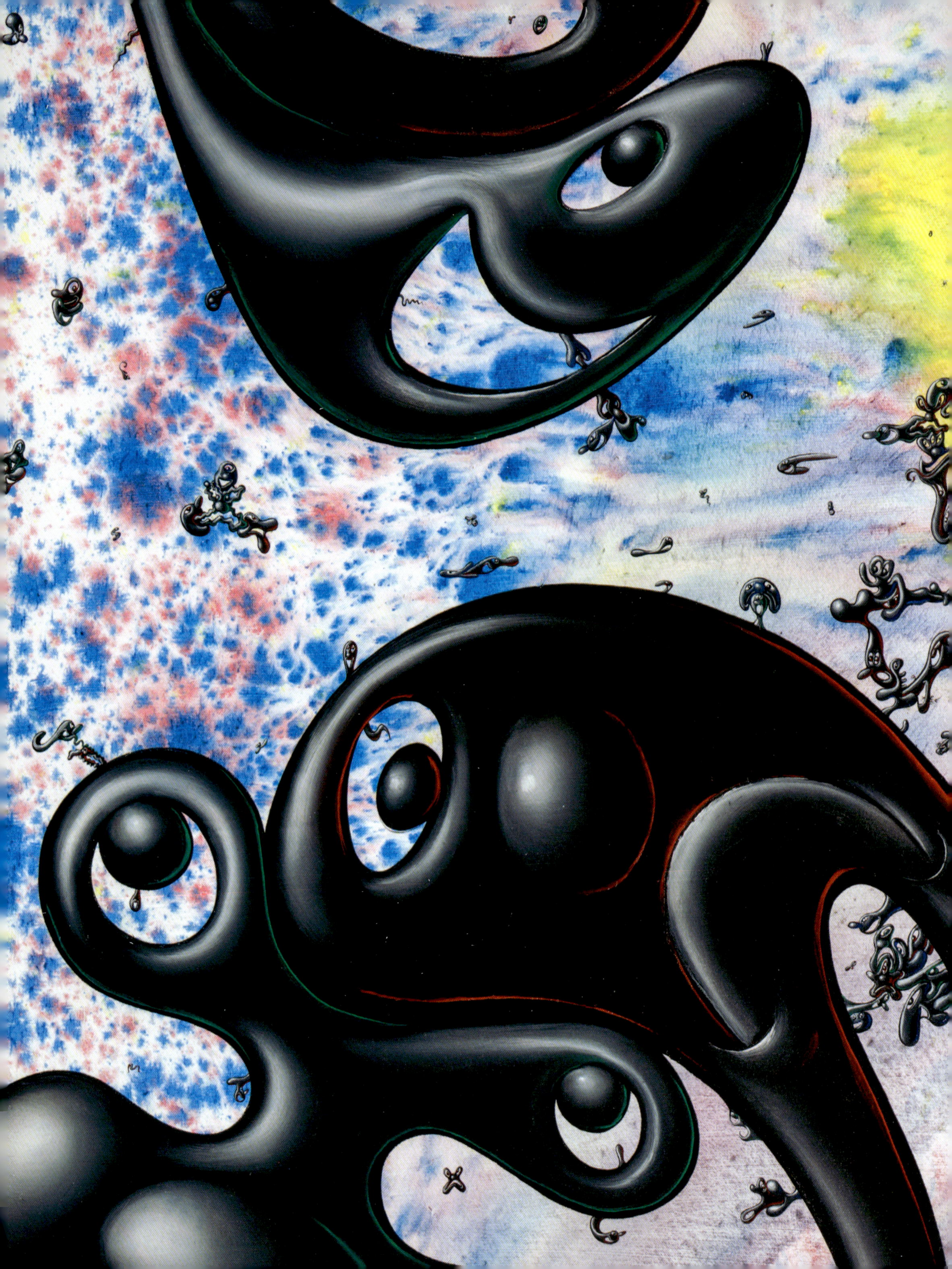

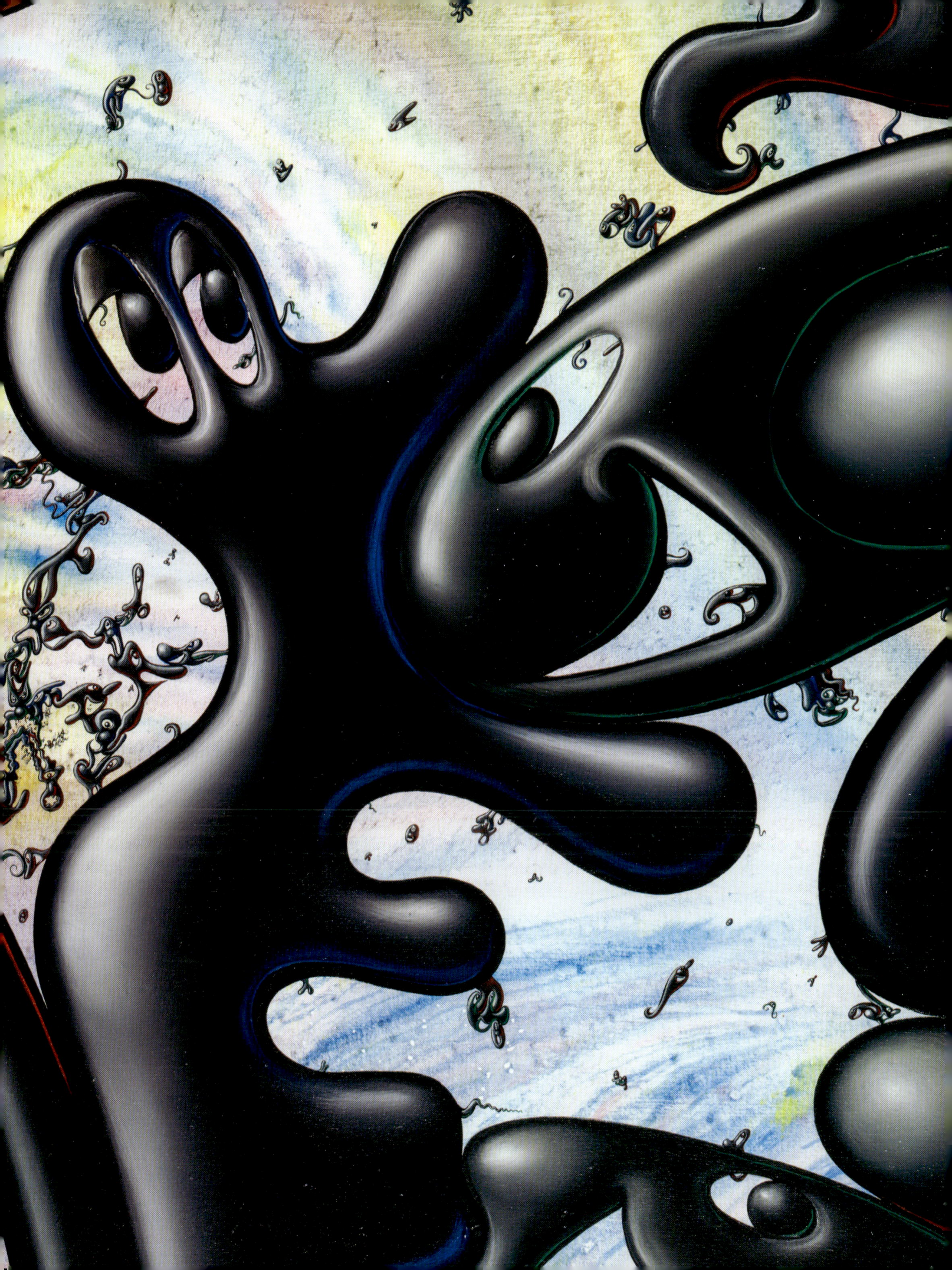

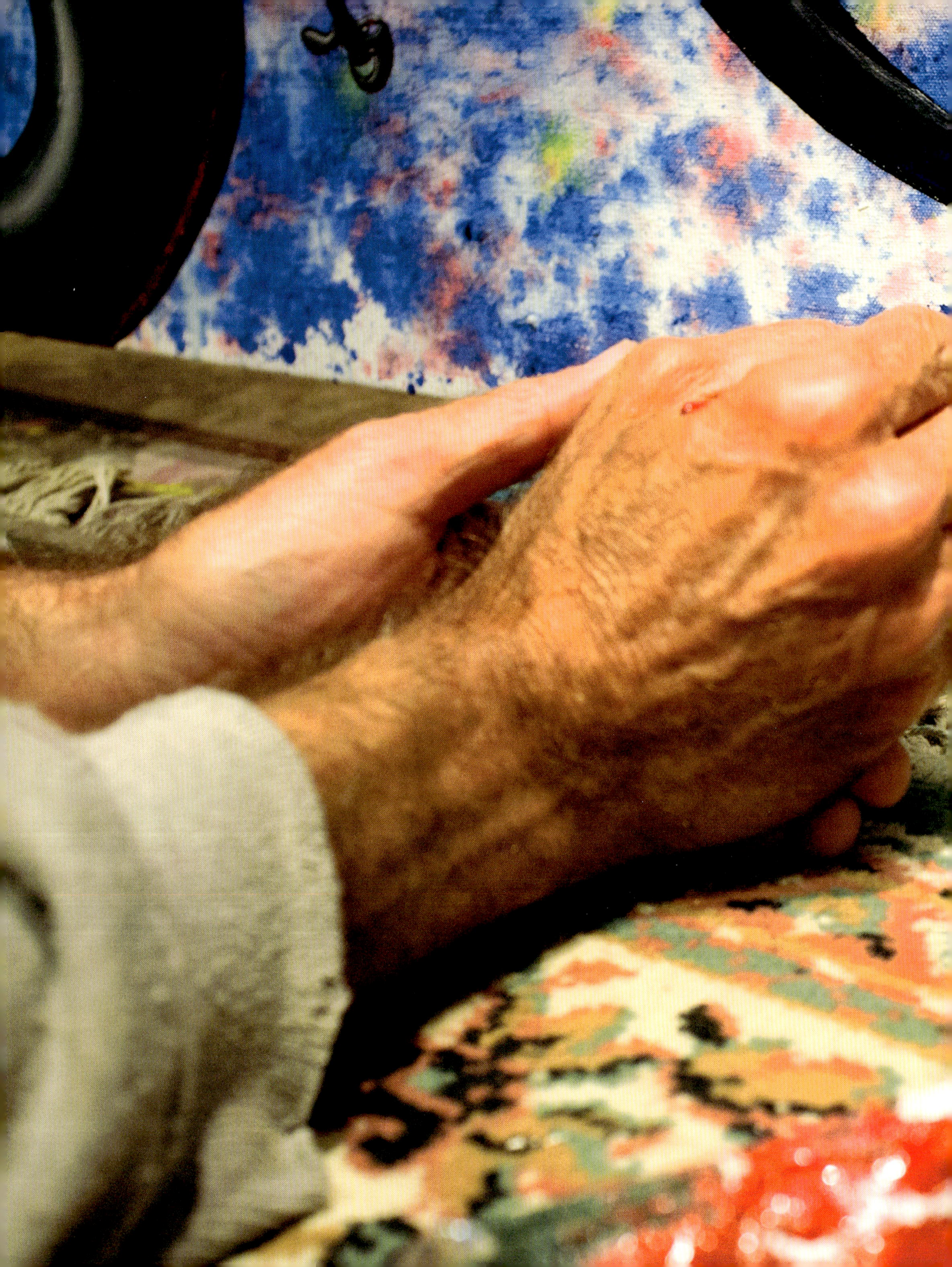

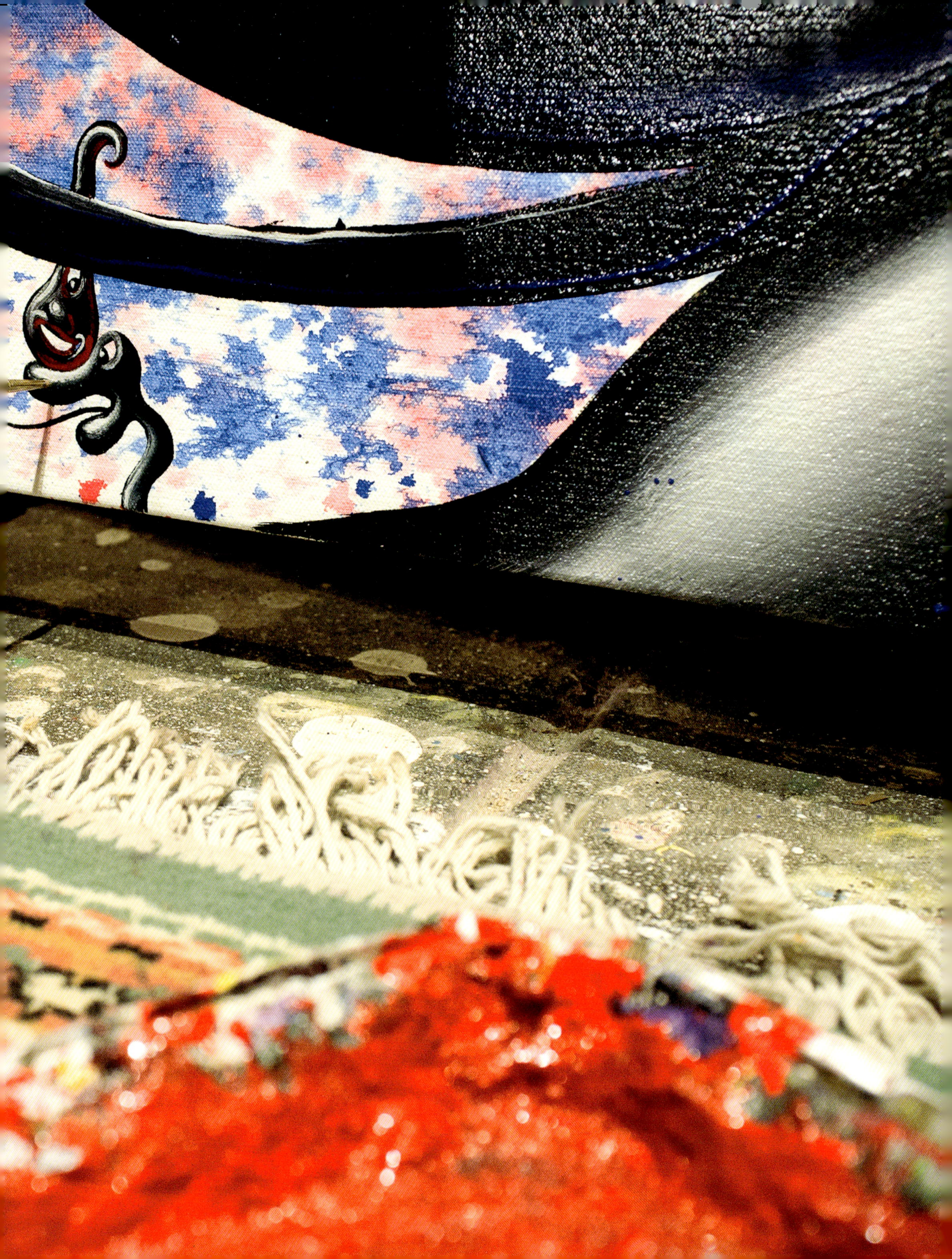

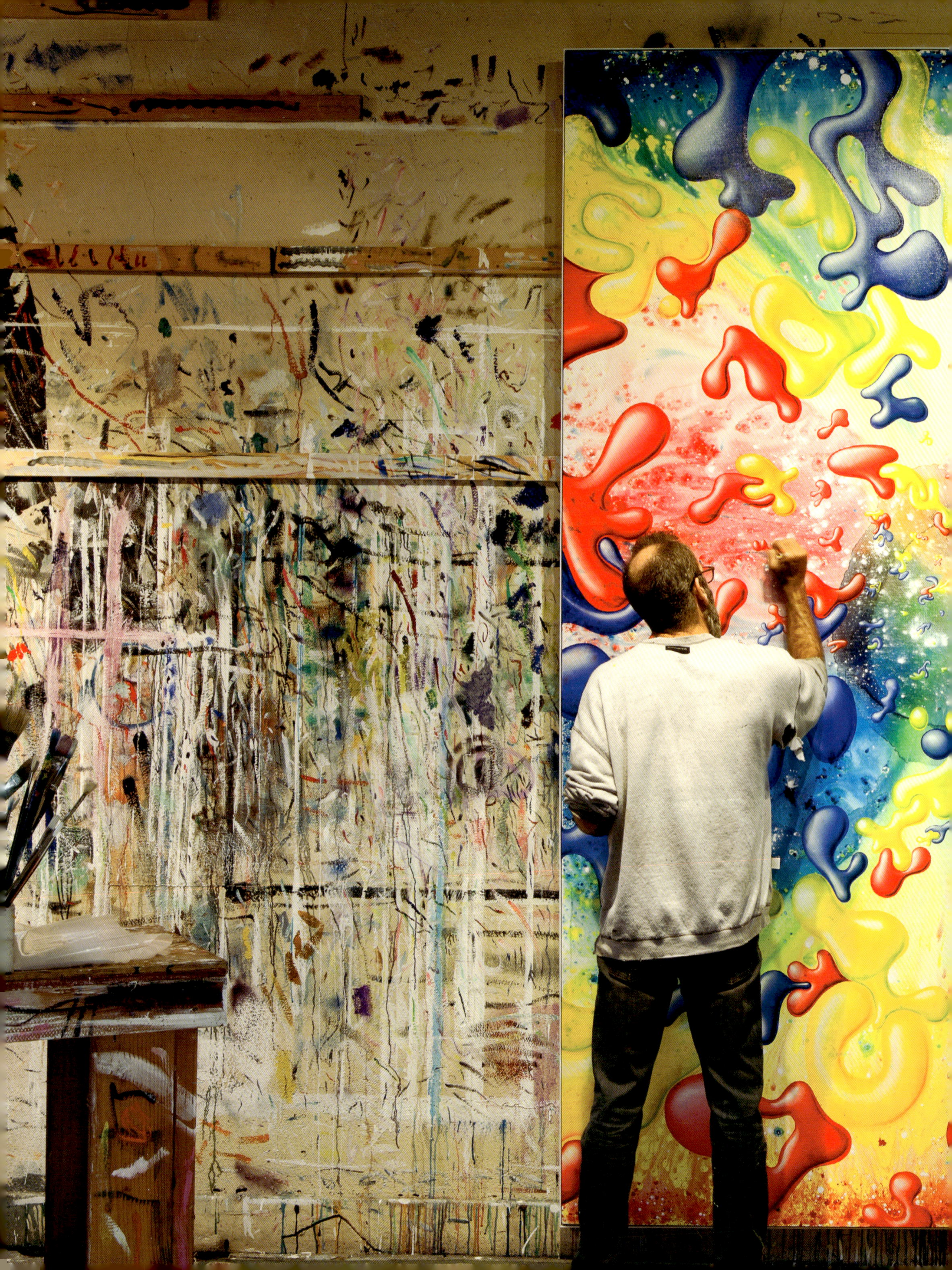

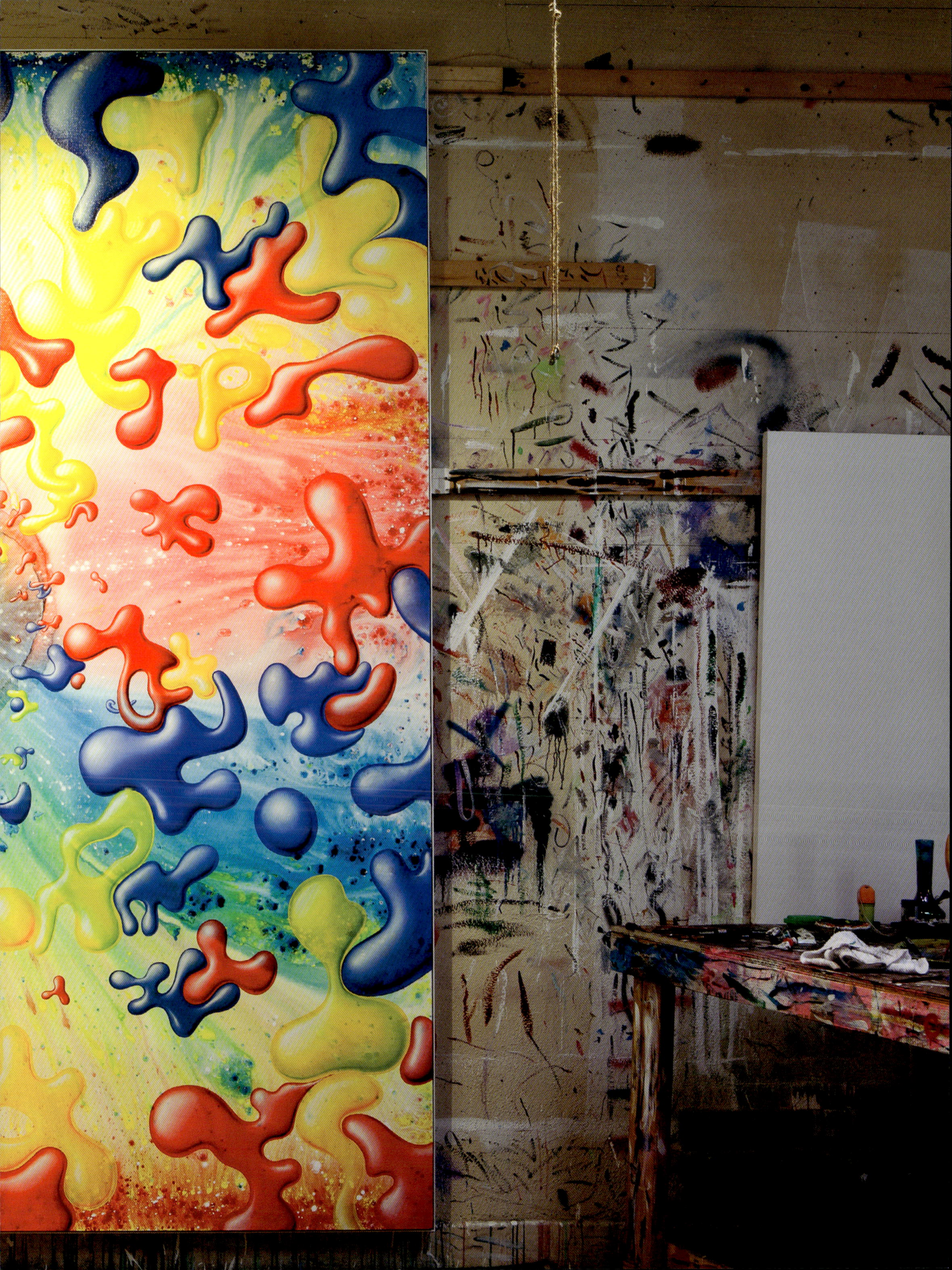

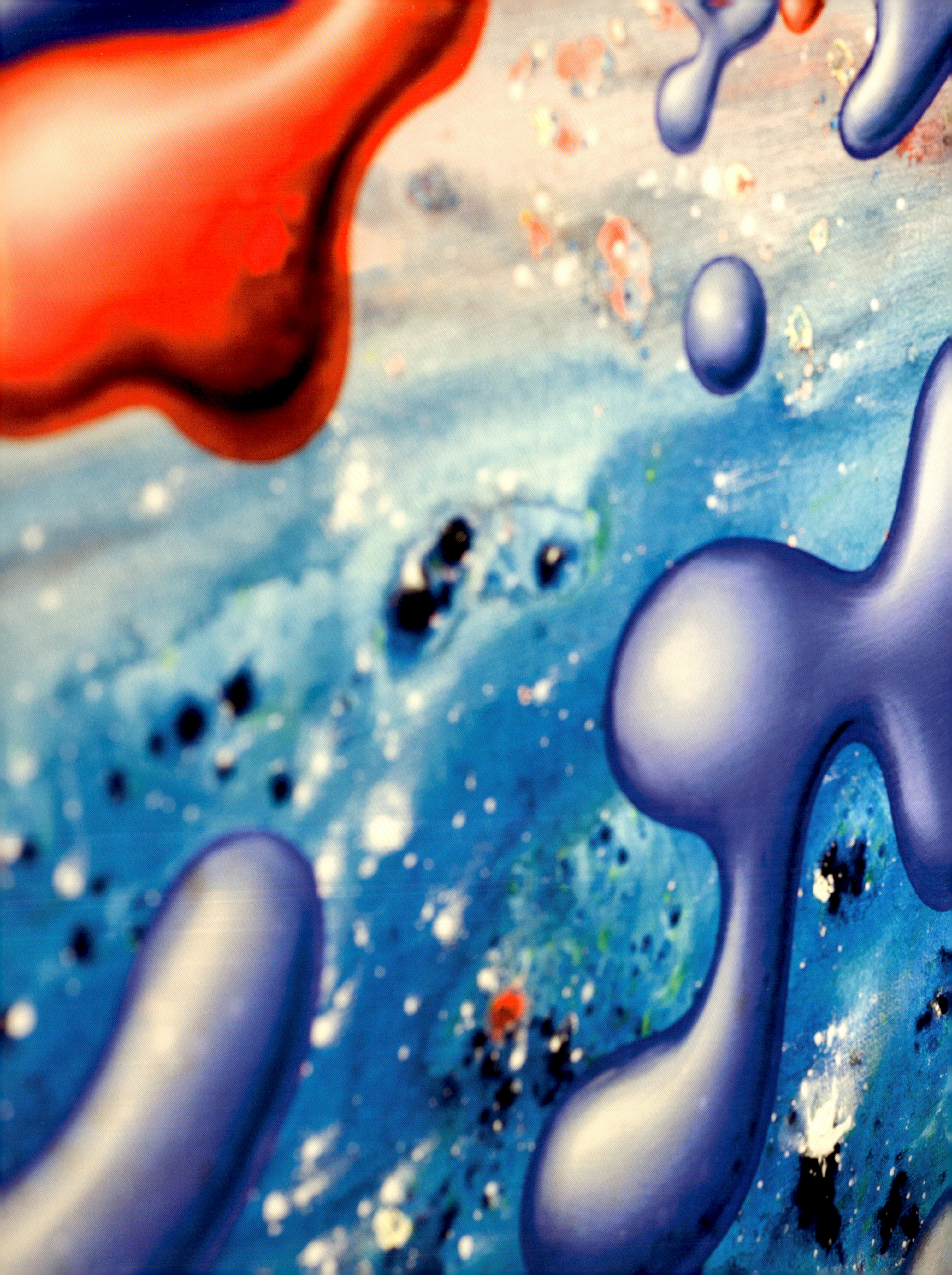

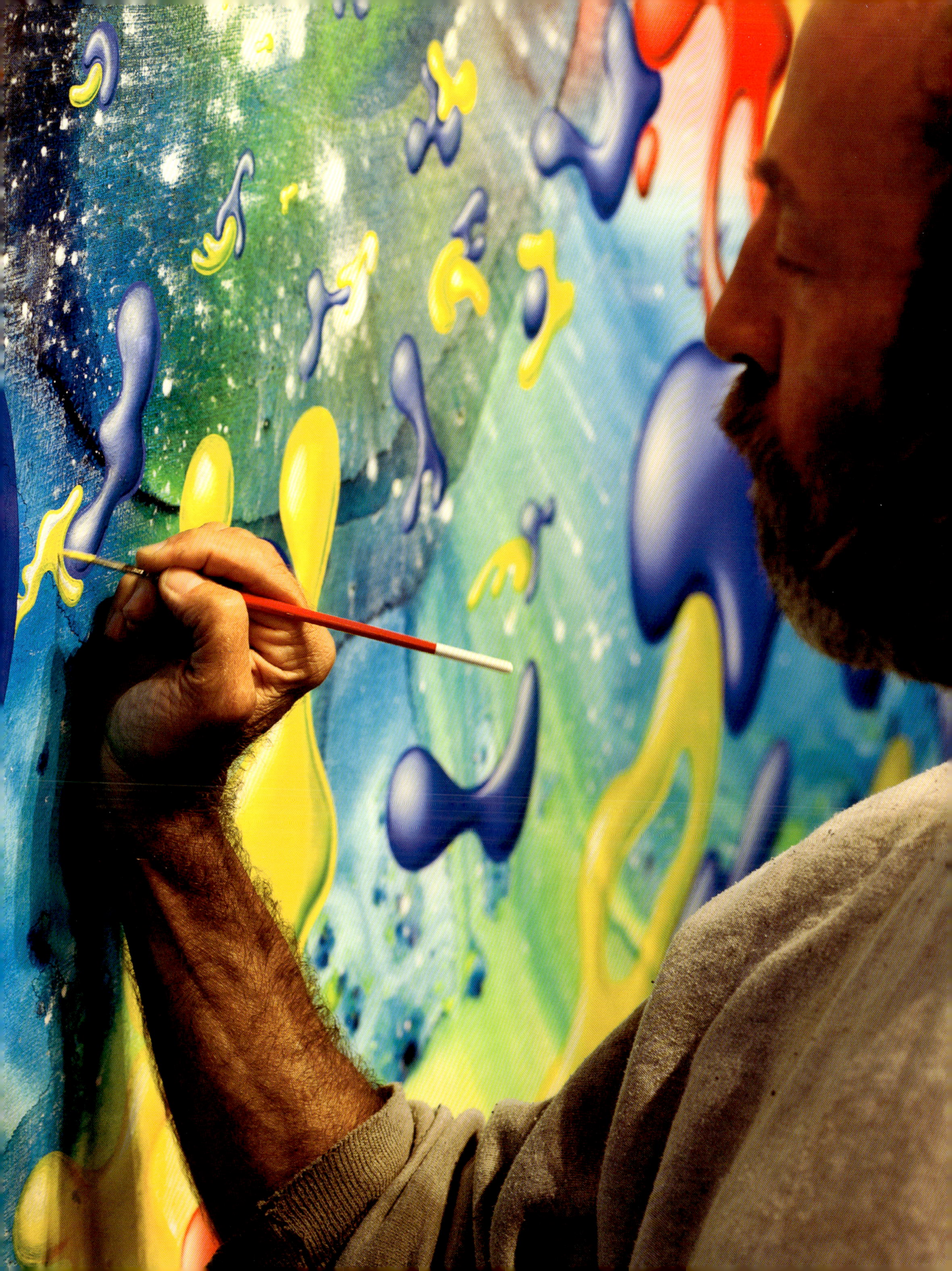

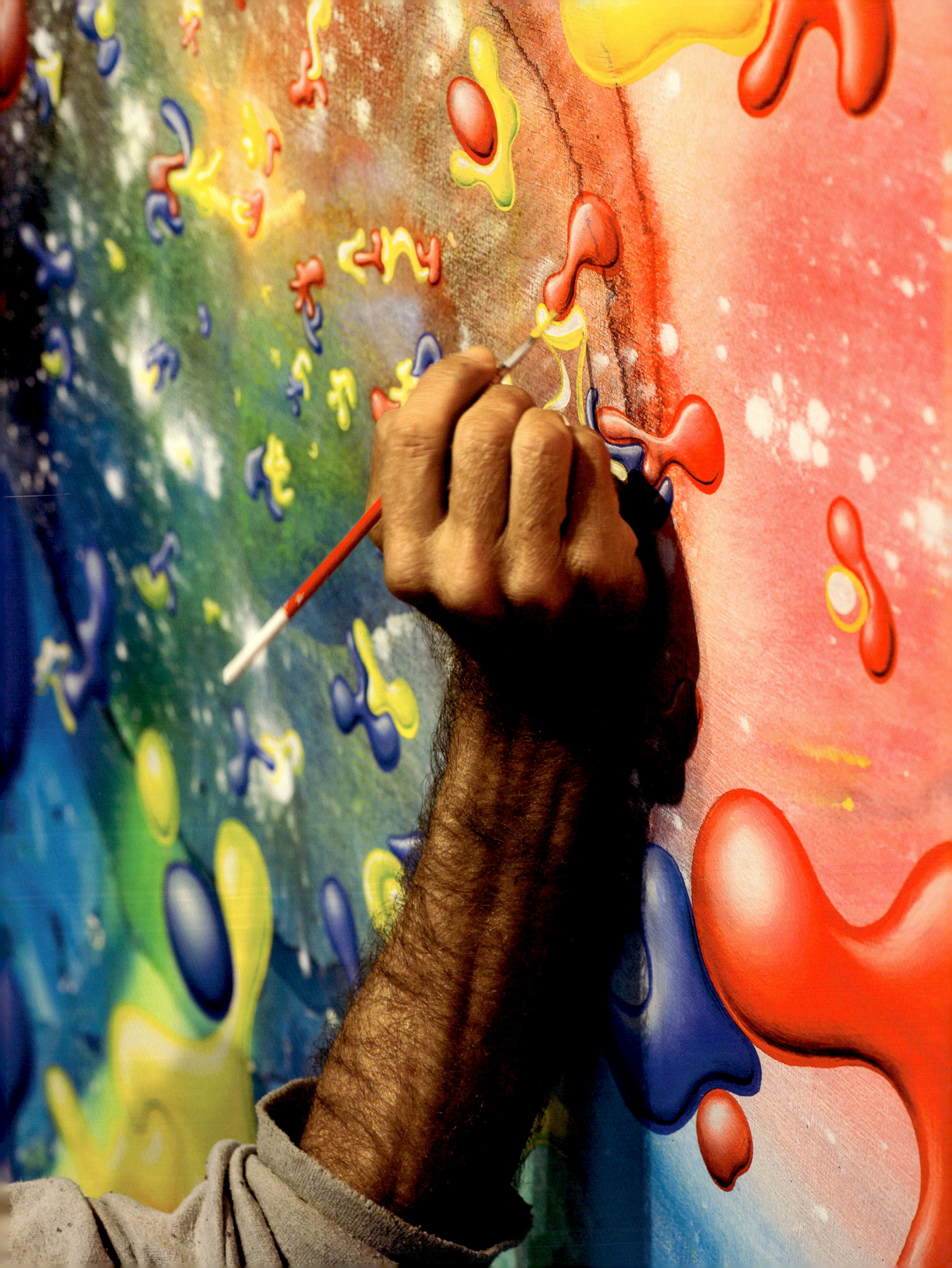

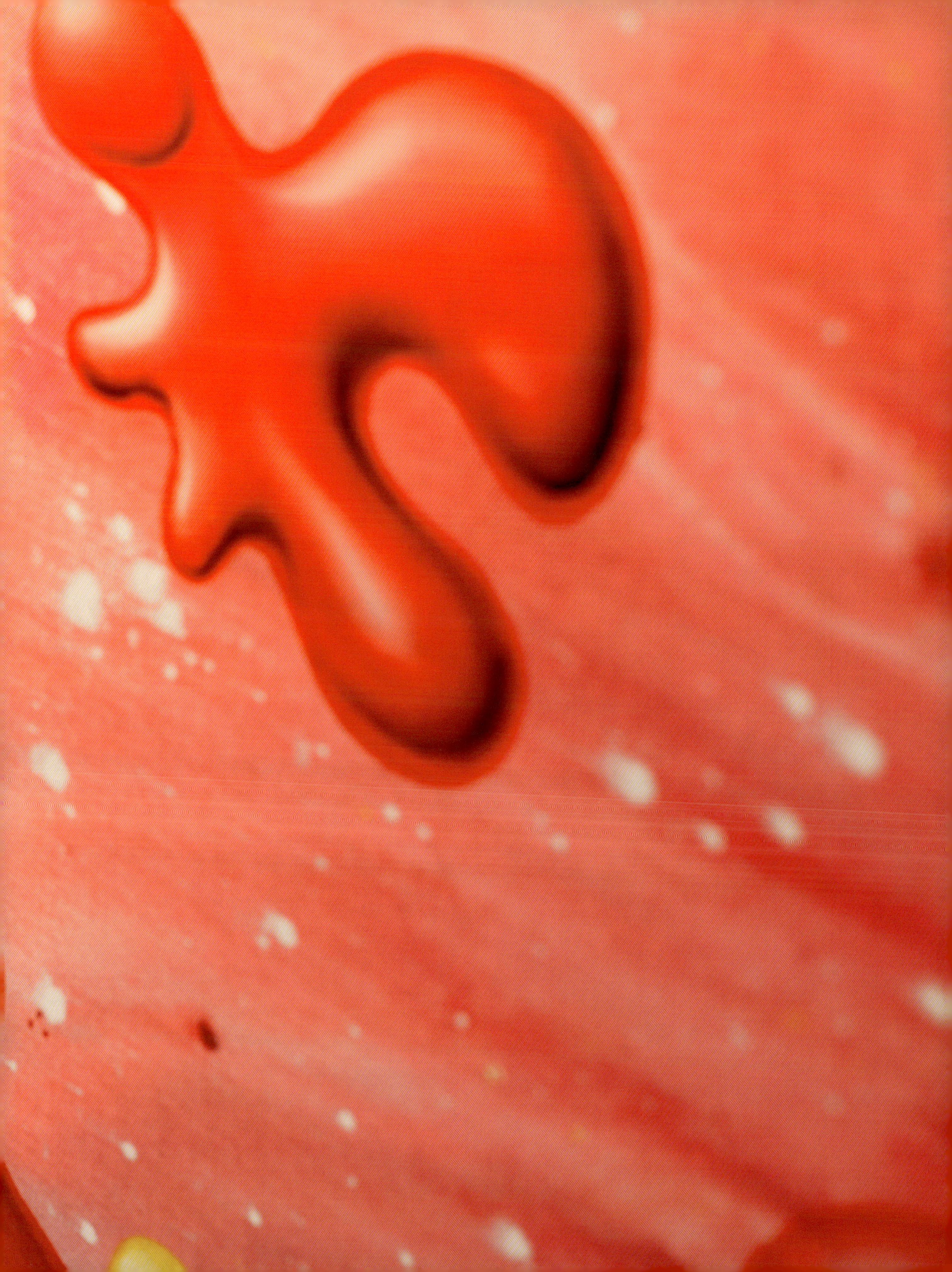

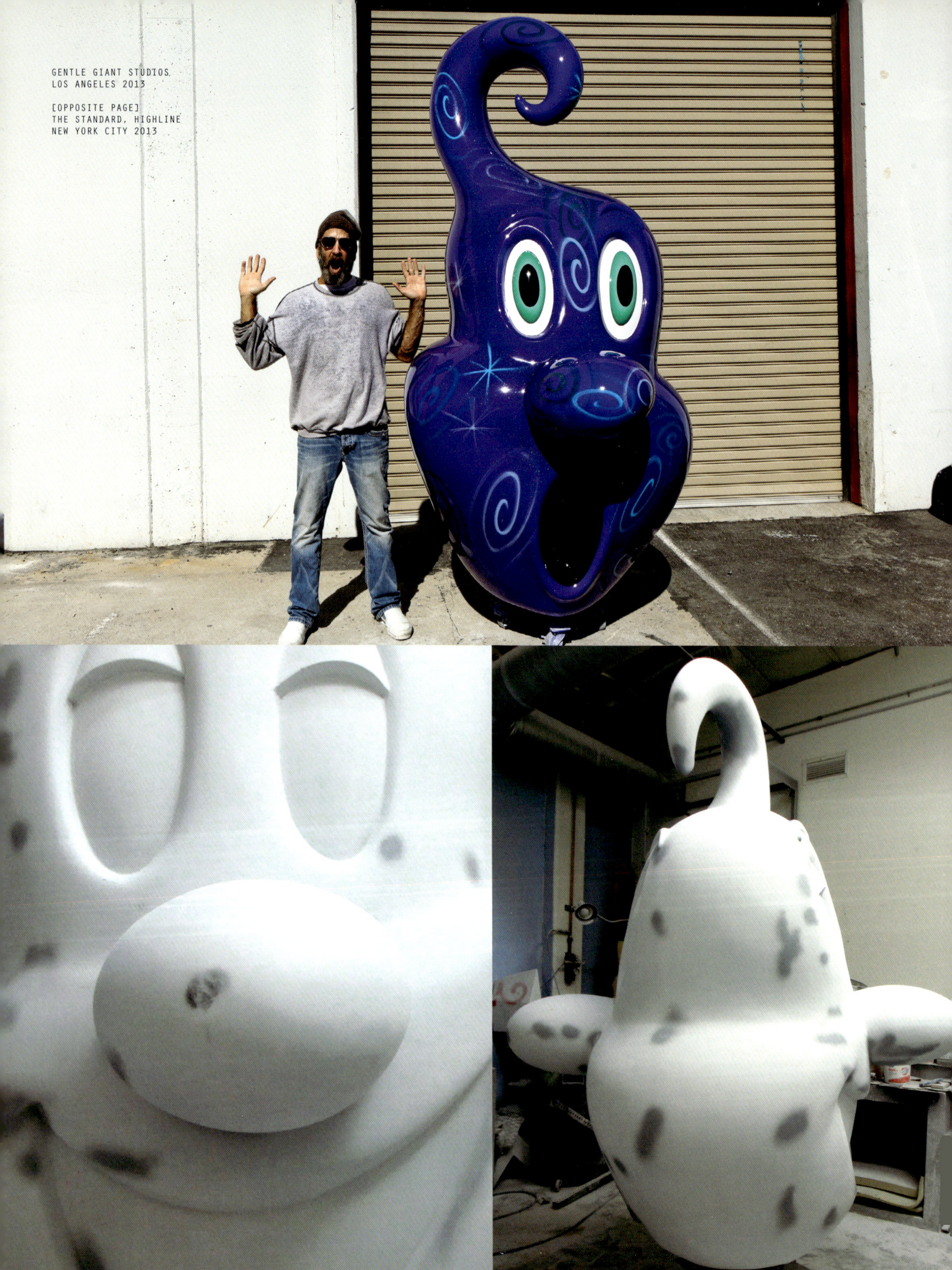

GENTLE GIANT STUDIOS
LOS ANGELES 2013

[OPPOSITE PAGE]
THE STANDARD, HIGHLINE
NEW YORK CITY 2013

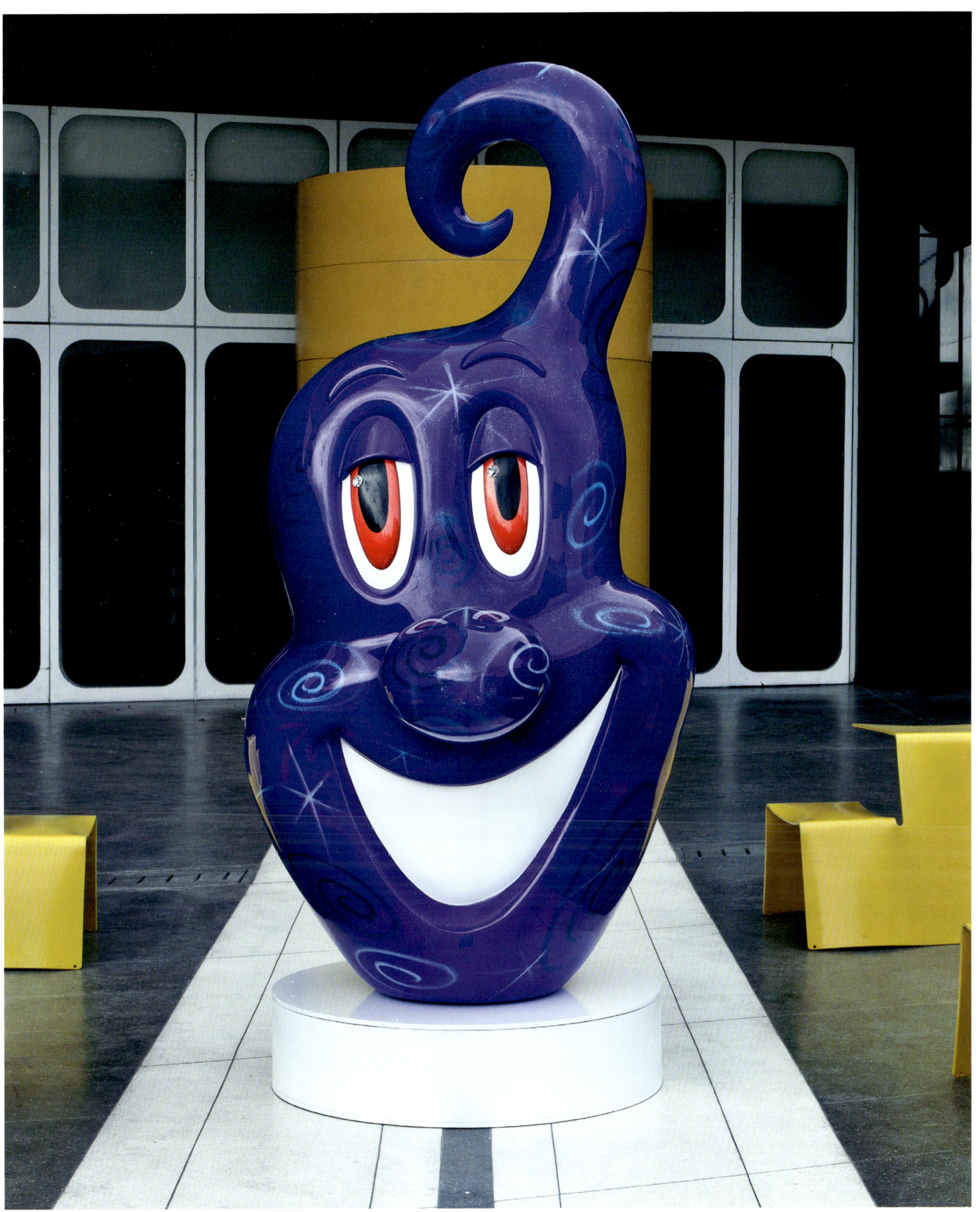

SQUIRTZ, 2013 - ENAMEL & RHINESTONE ON FIBERGLASS / 96 X 48.5 X 74.5 INCHES

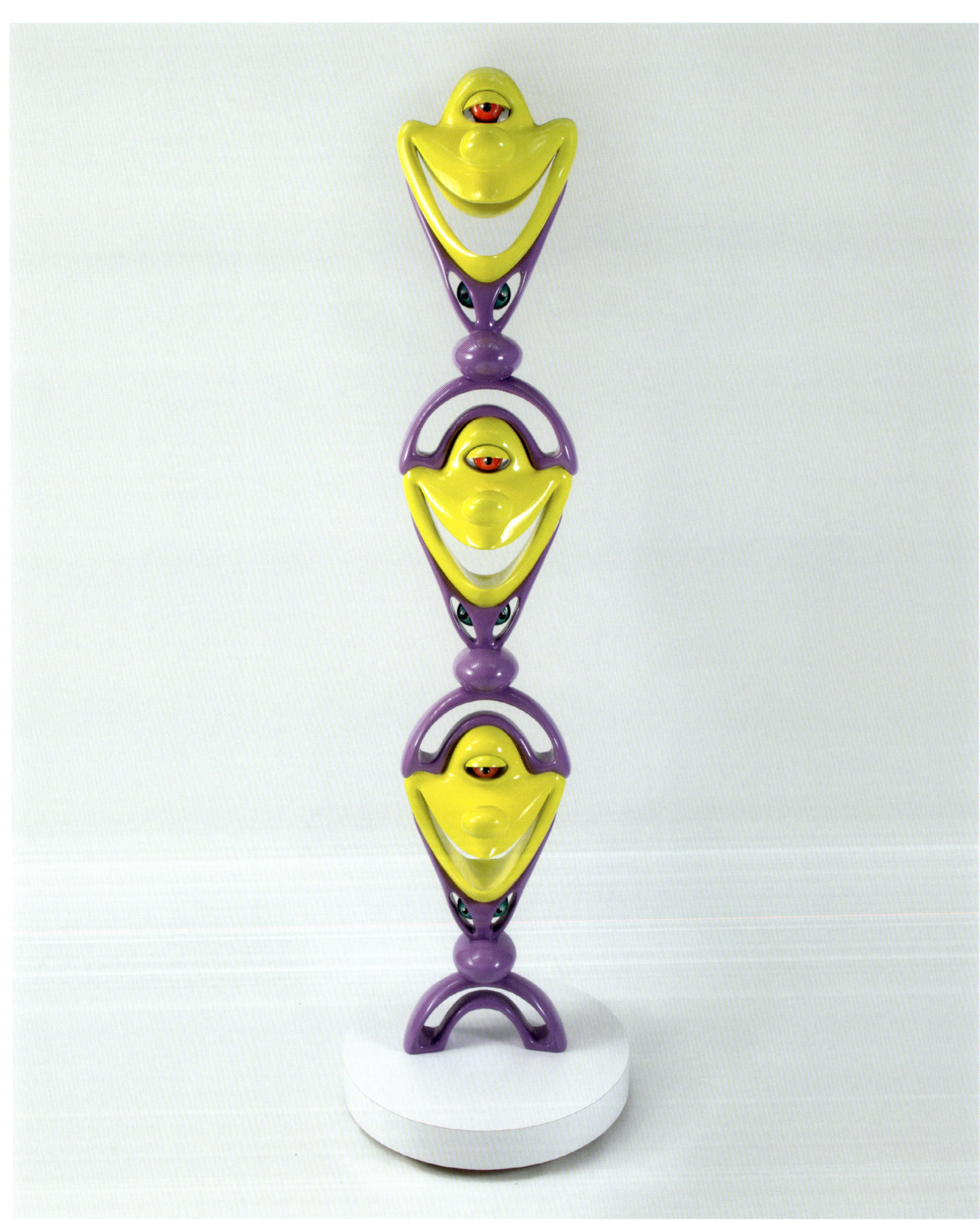

TOTEMOTIKI, 2013 - ENAMEL & RHINESTONE ON FIBERGLASS / 144 X 27 X 30 INCHES

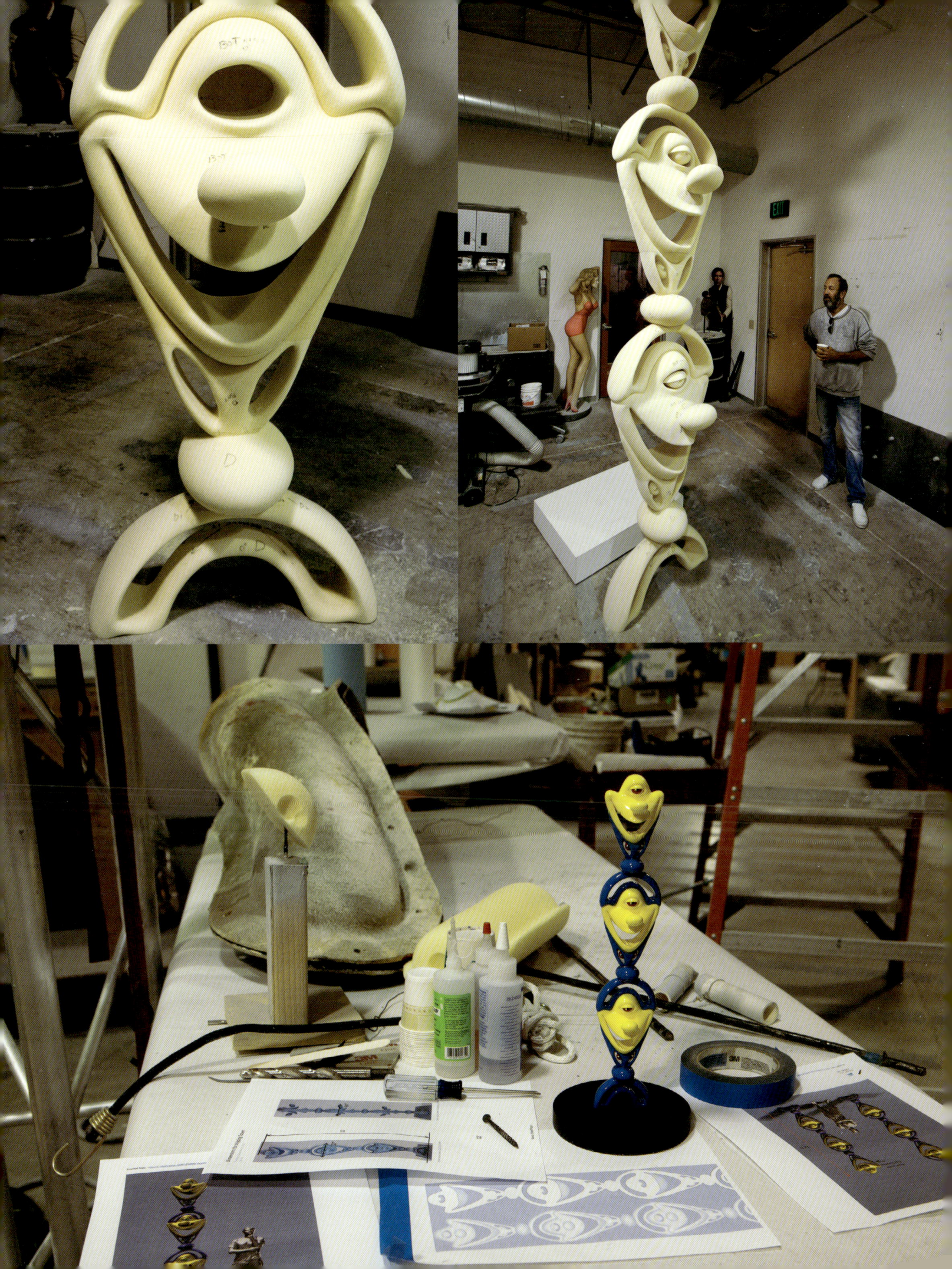

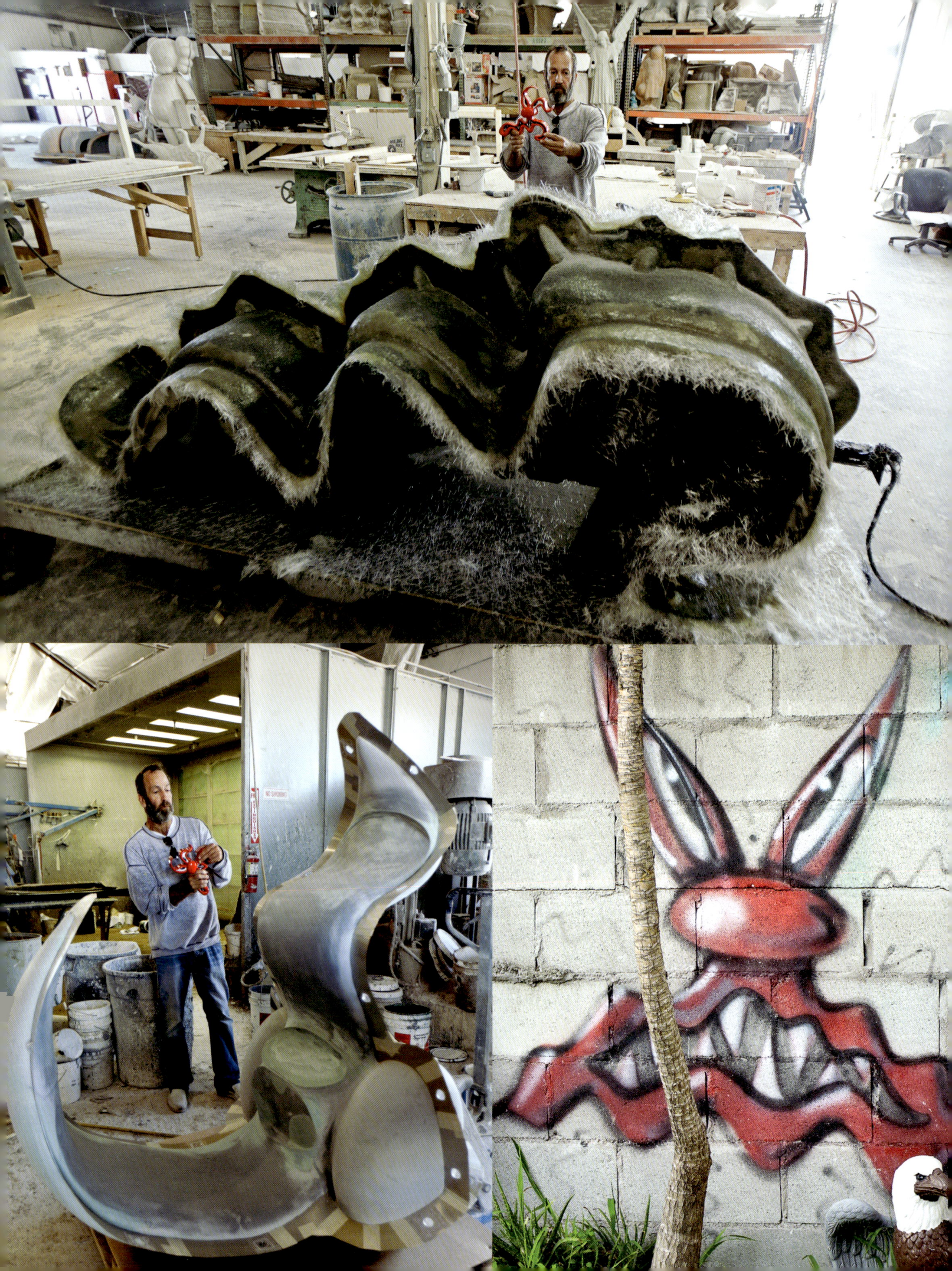

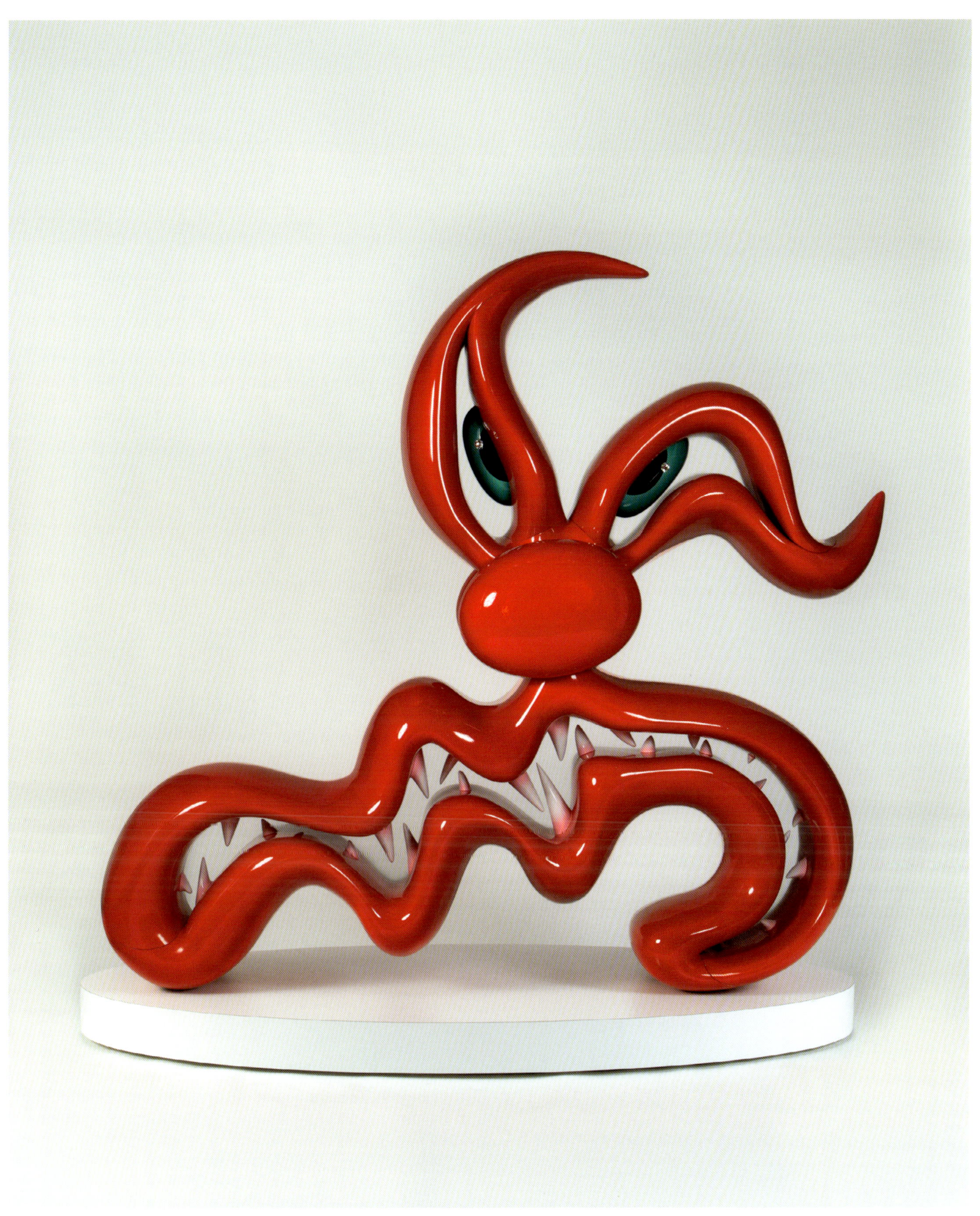

RED SCARY GUY, 2013 - ENAMEL & RHINESTONE ON FIBERGLASS / 96 X 103.5 X 36.5 INCHES

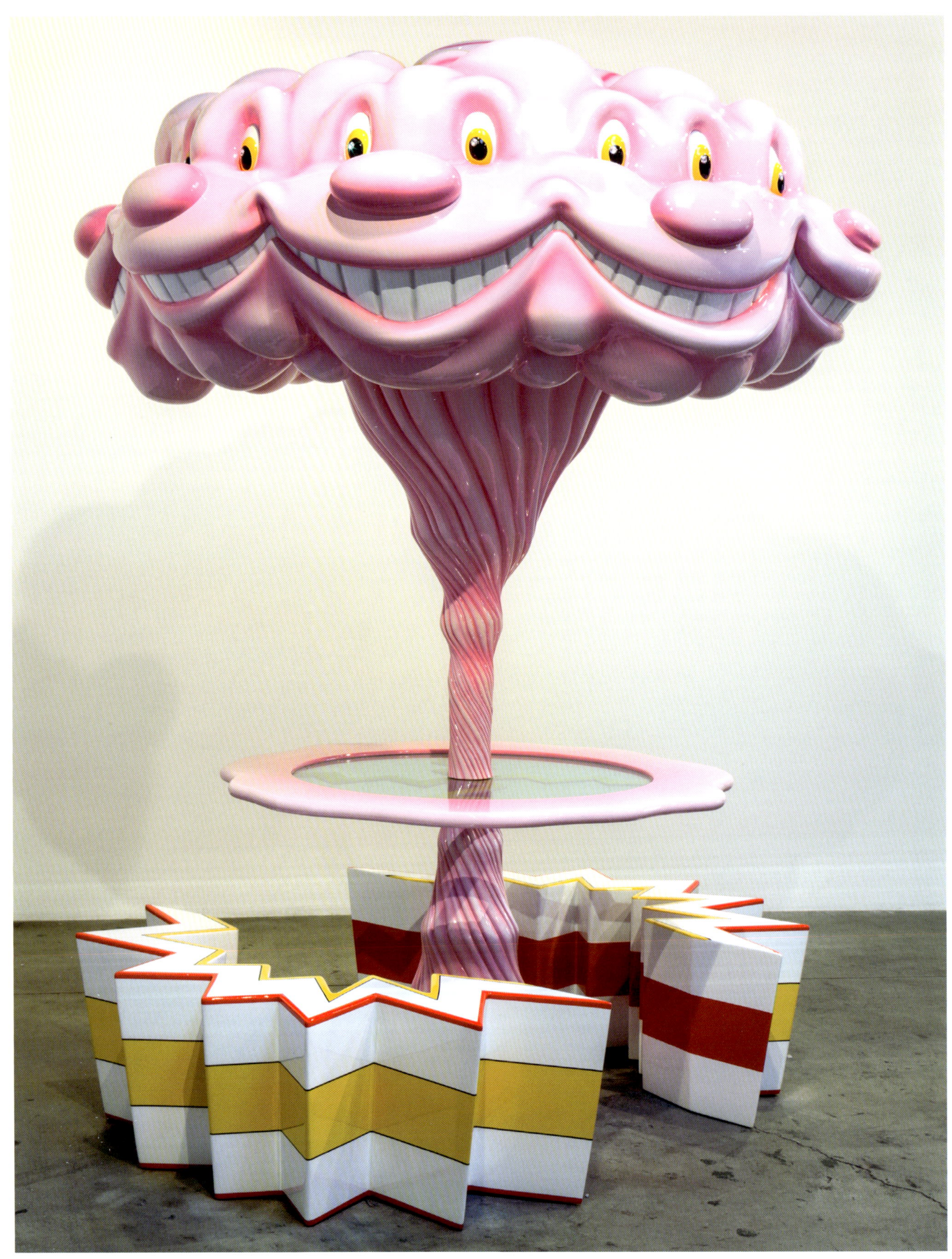

PIKABOOM!, 2012 - FIBERGLASS, STEEL & ENAMEL / 108 X 80 X 80 INCHES

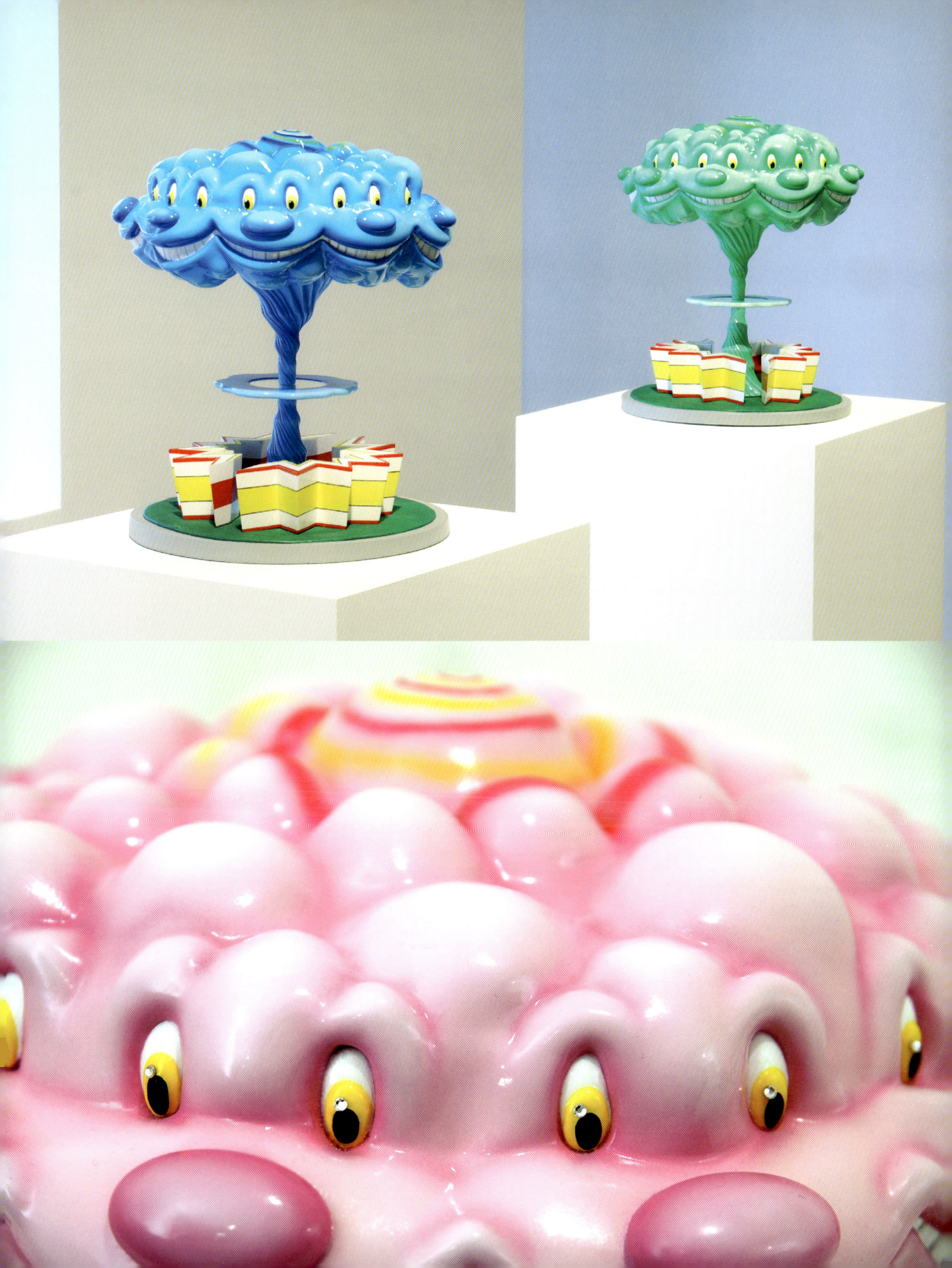

MURALS

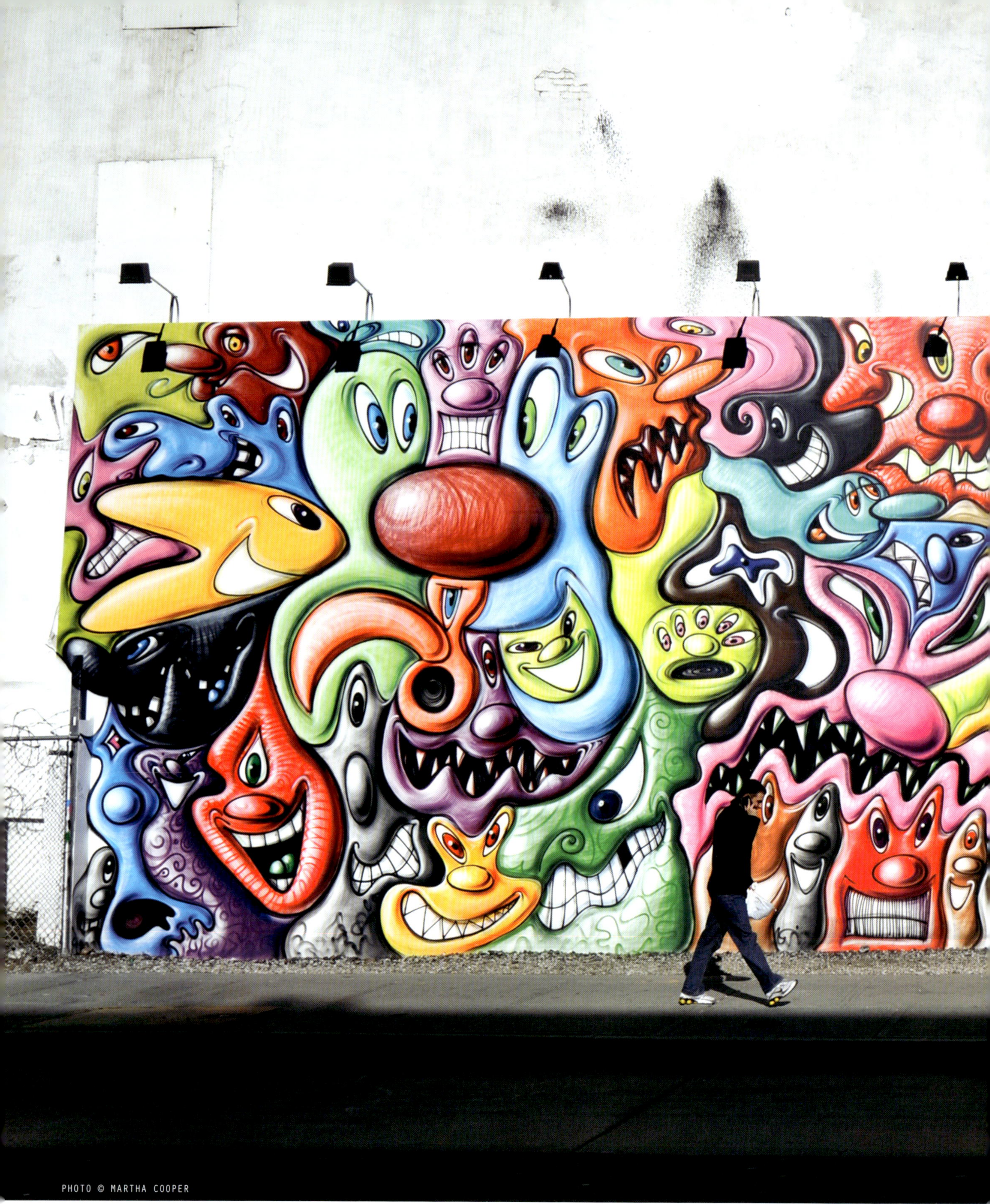

PHOTO © MARTHA COOPER

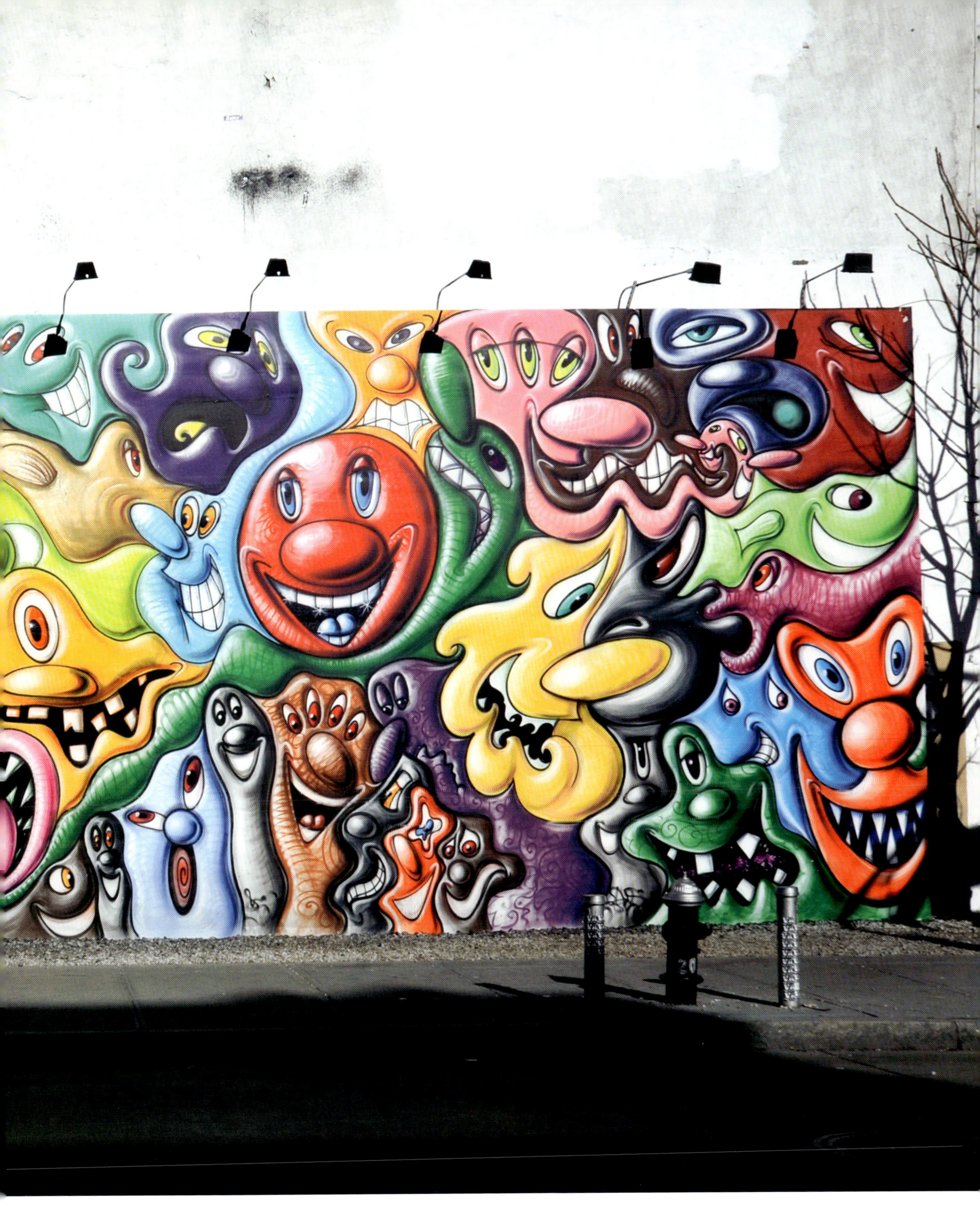

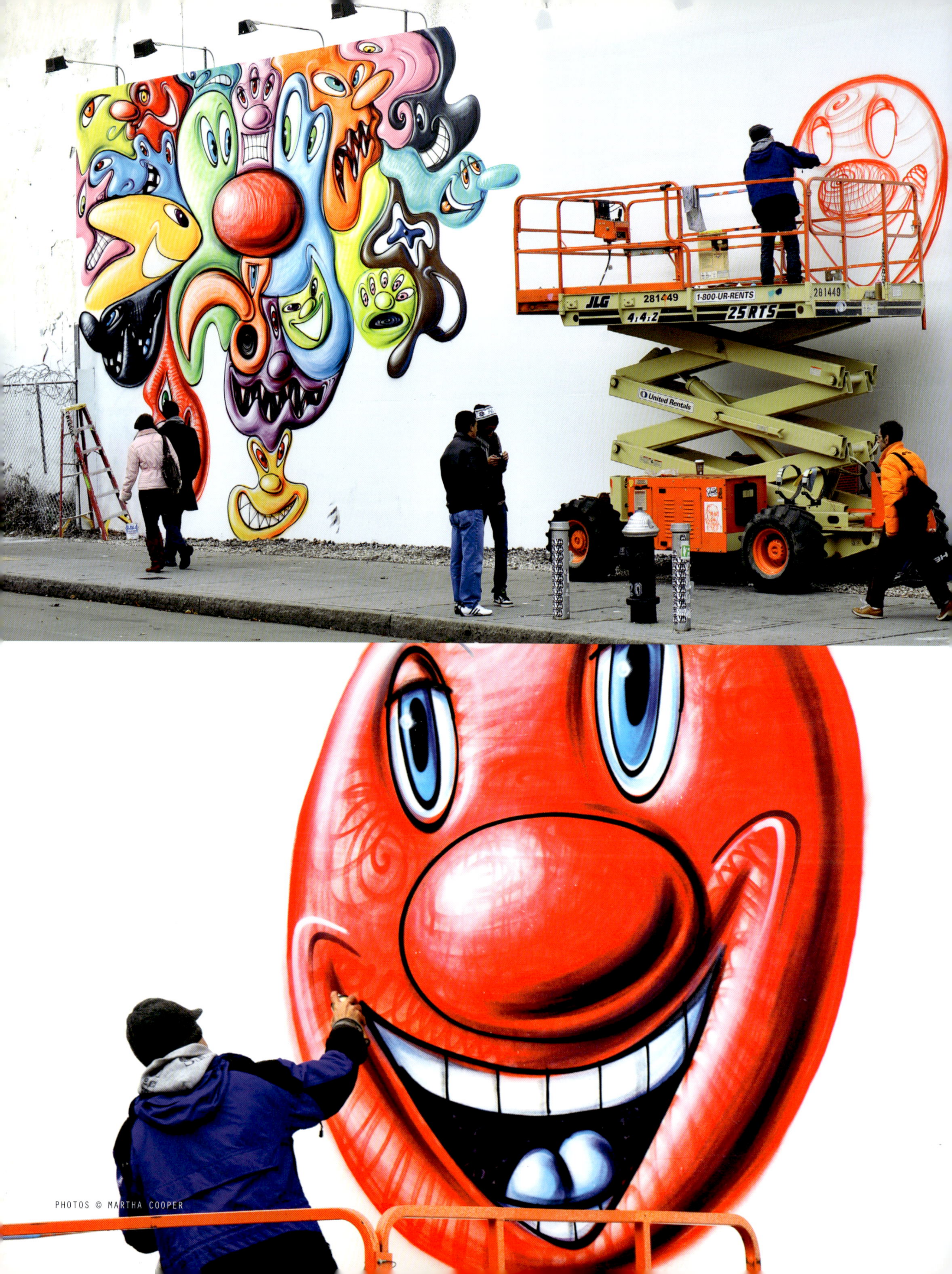

PHOTOS © MARTHA COOPER

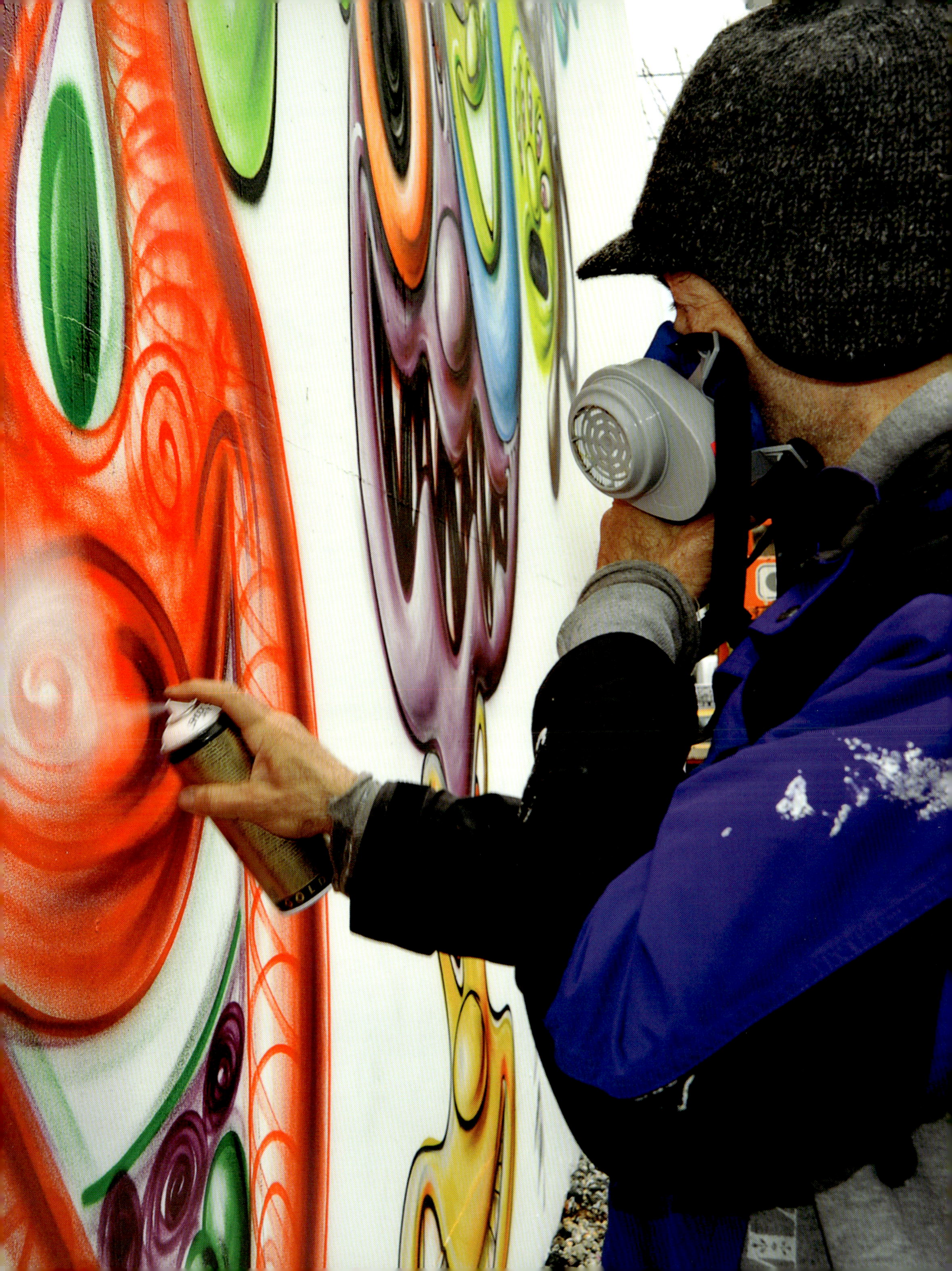

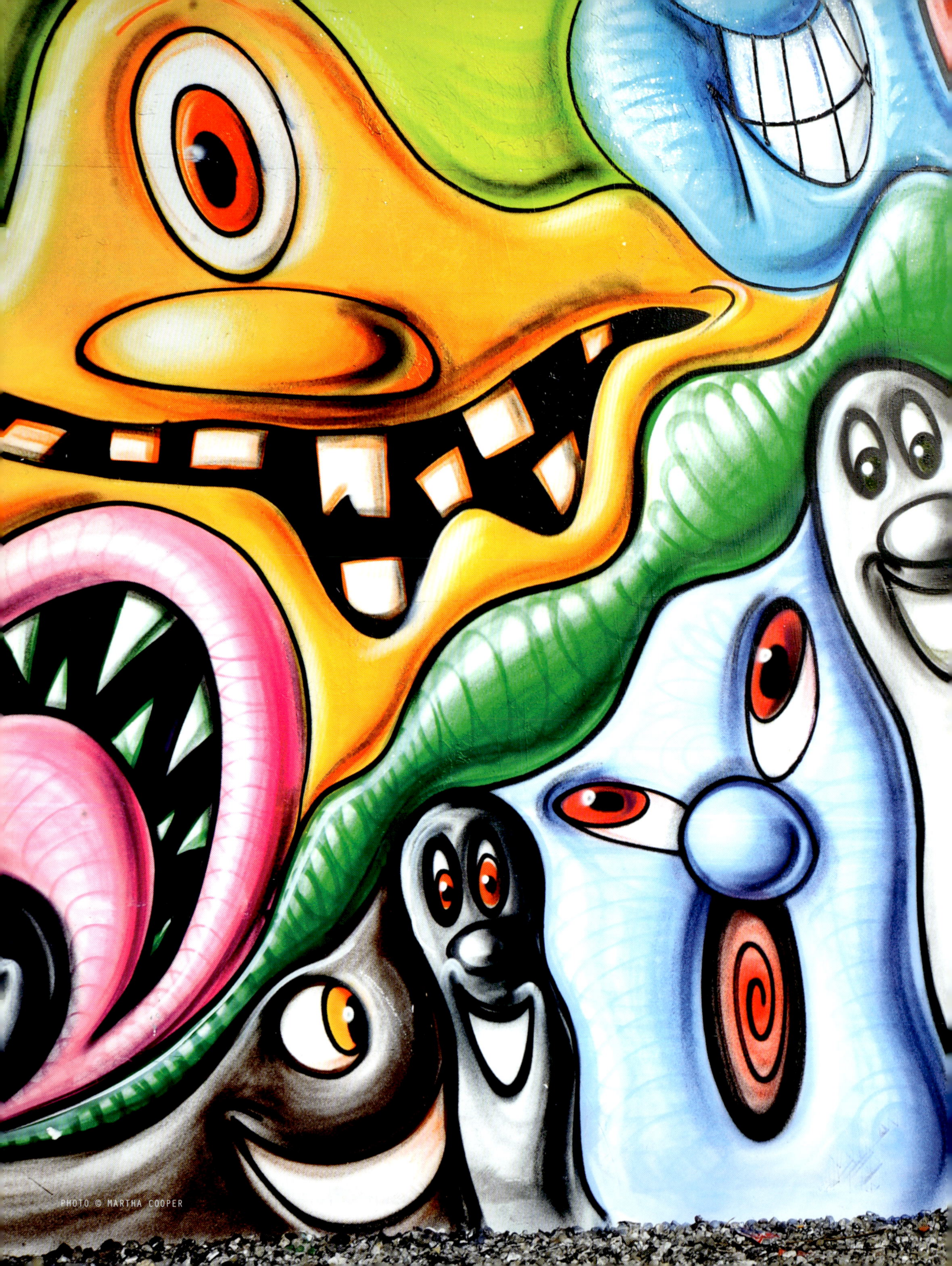

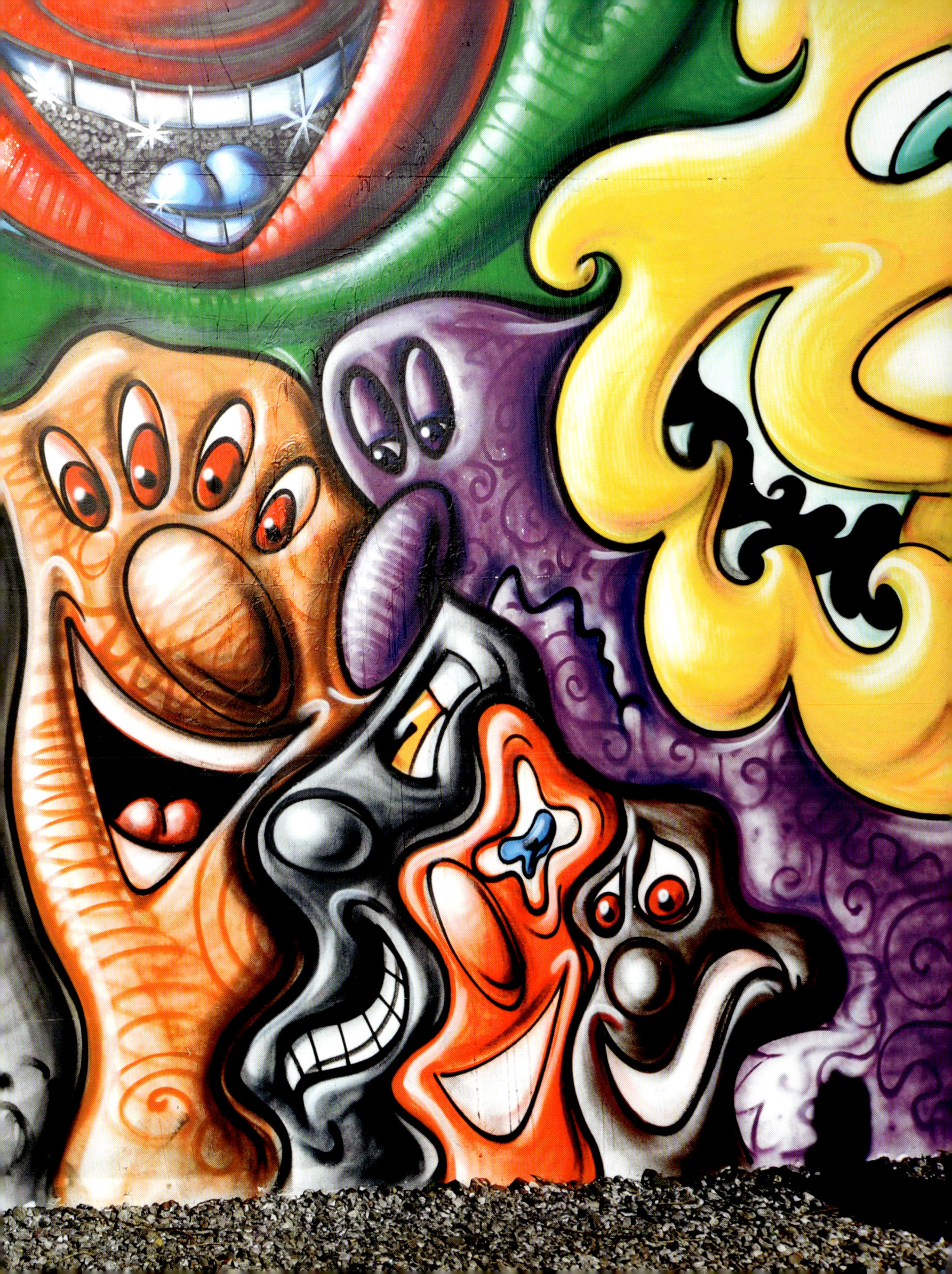

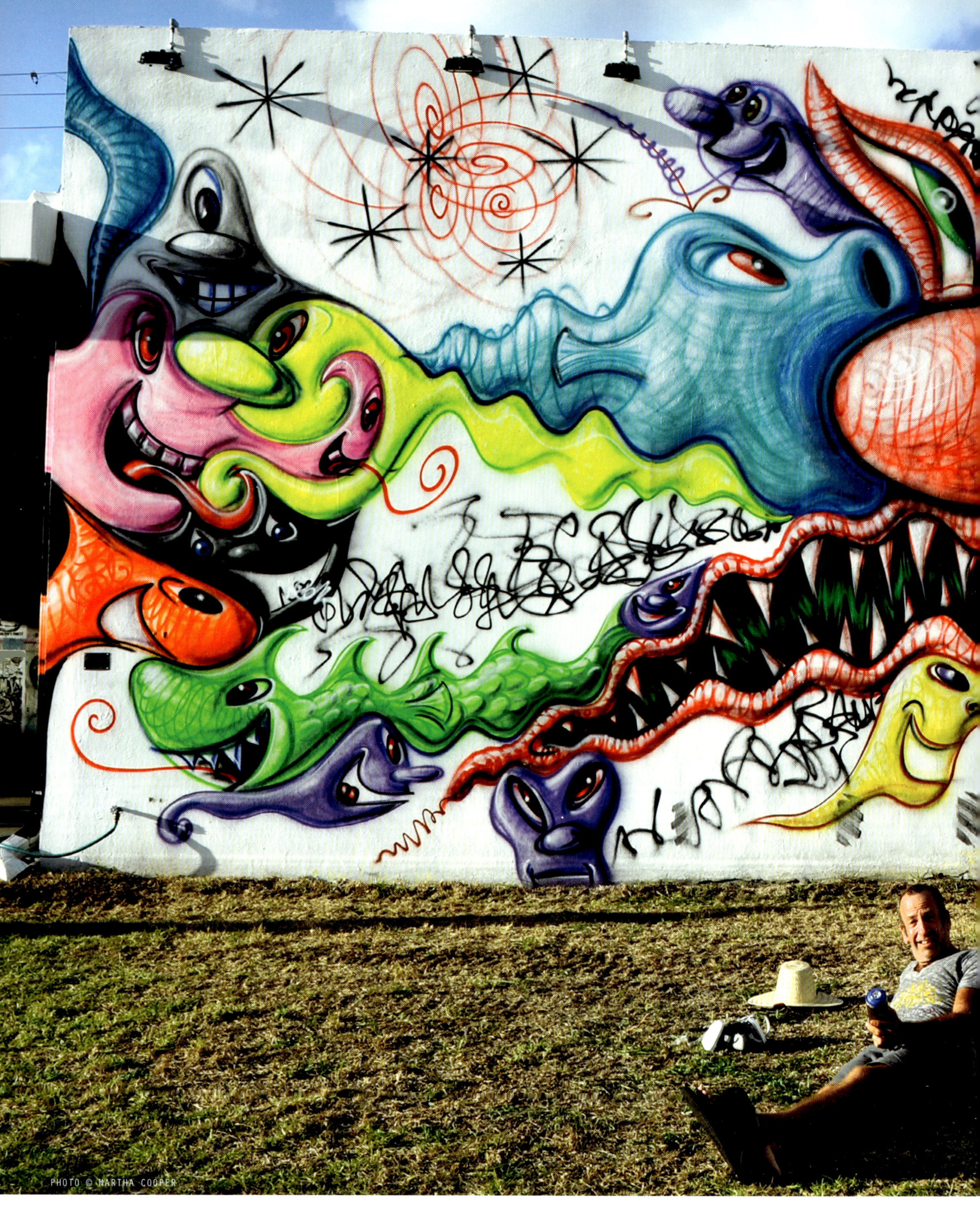
PHOTO © MARTHA COOPER

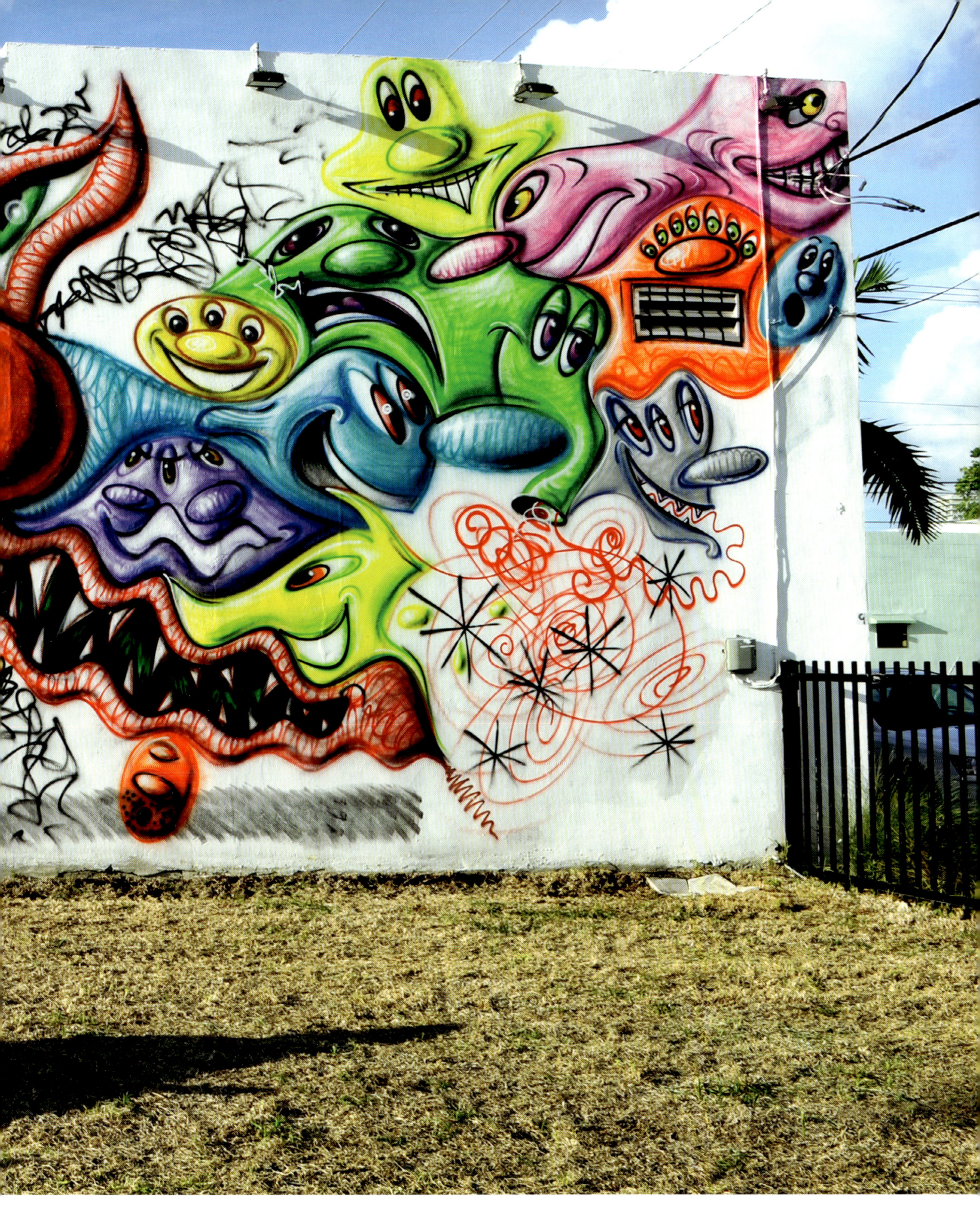

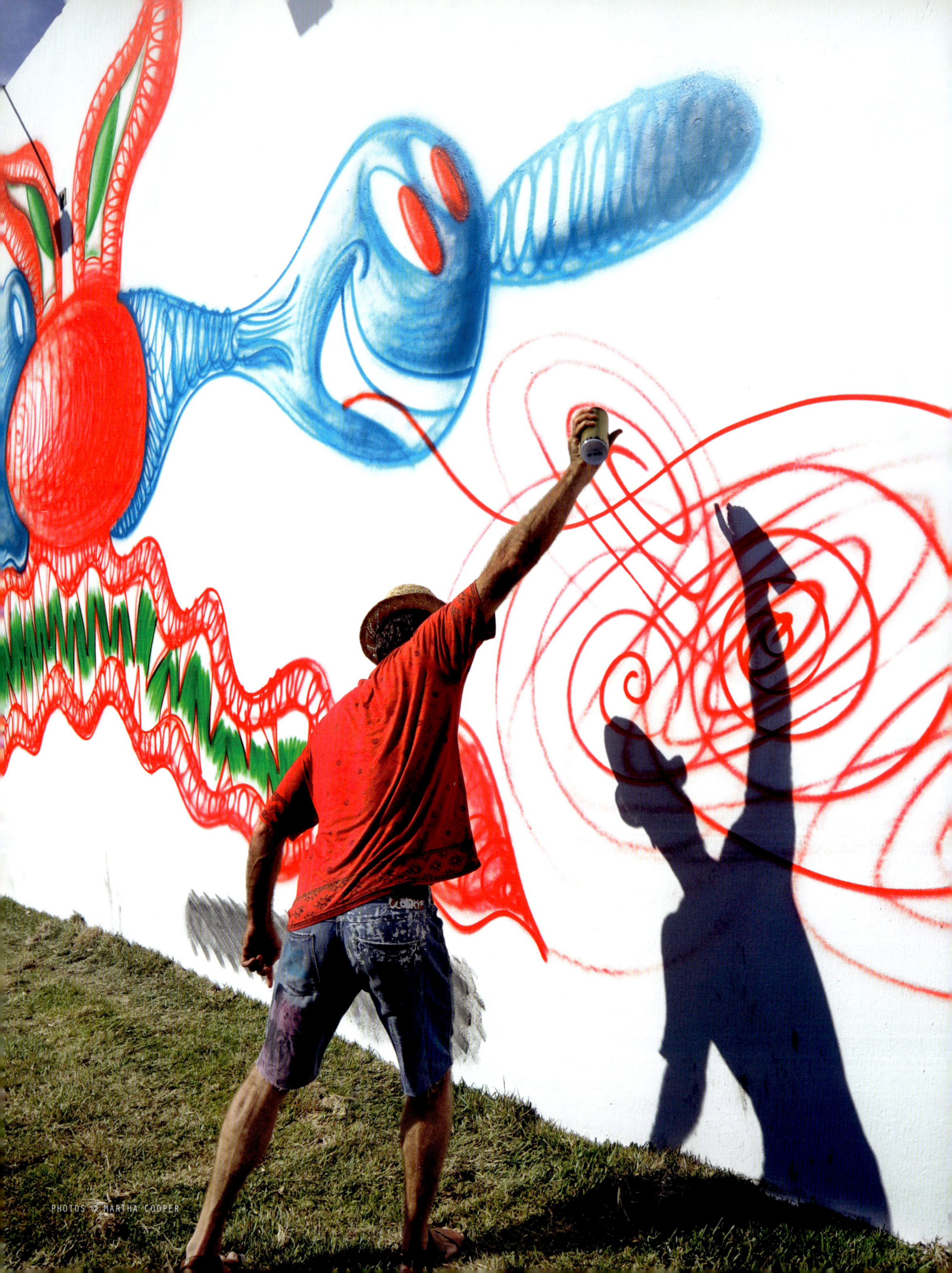

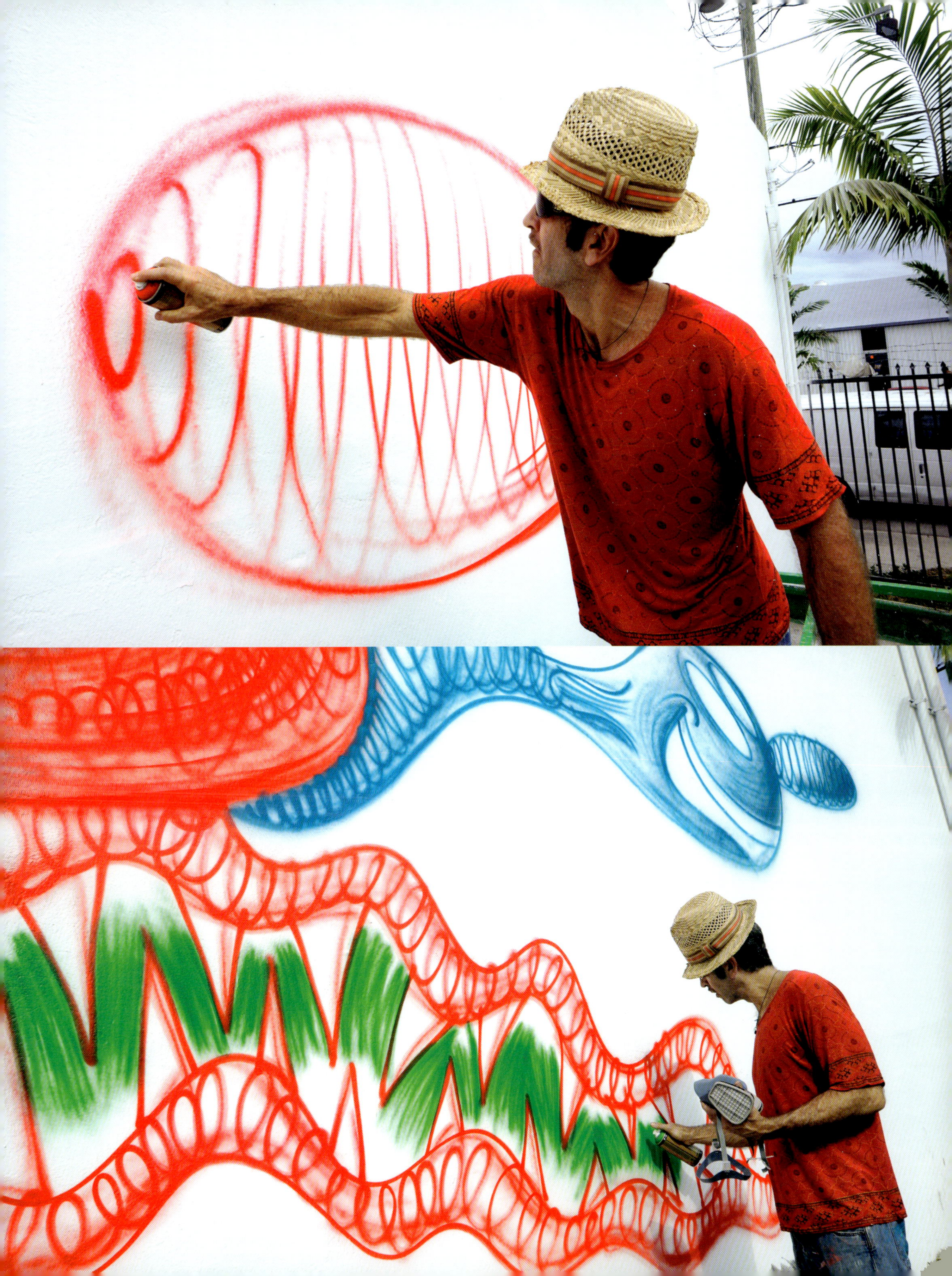

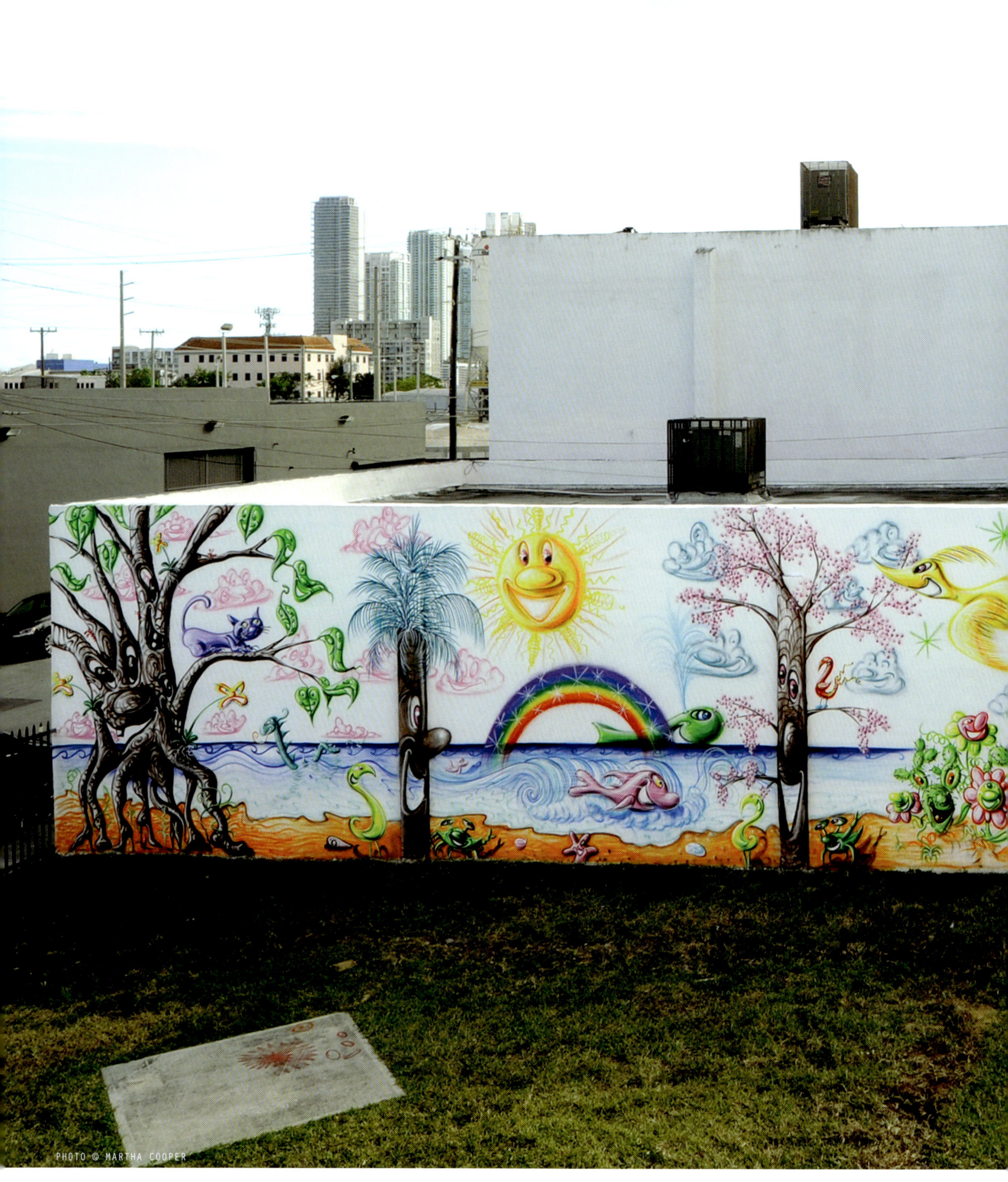

PHOTO © MARTHA COOPER

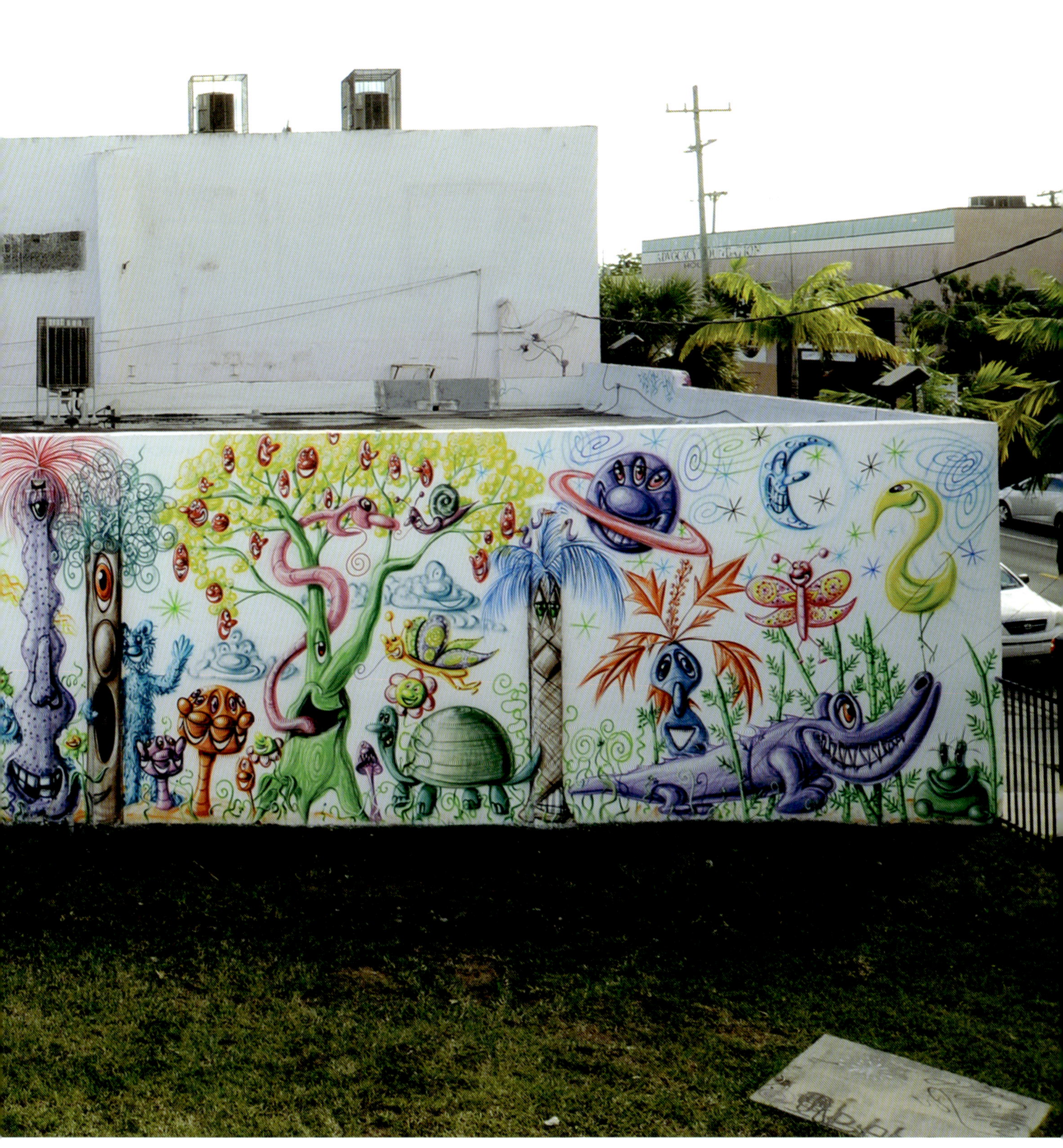

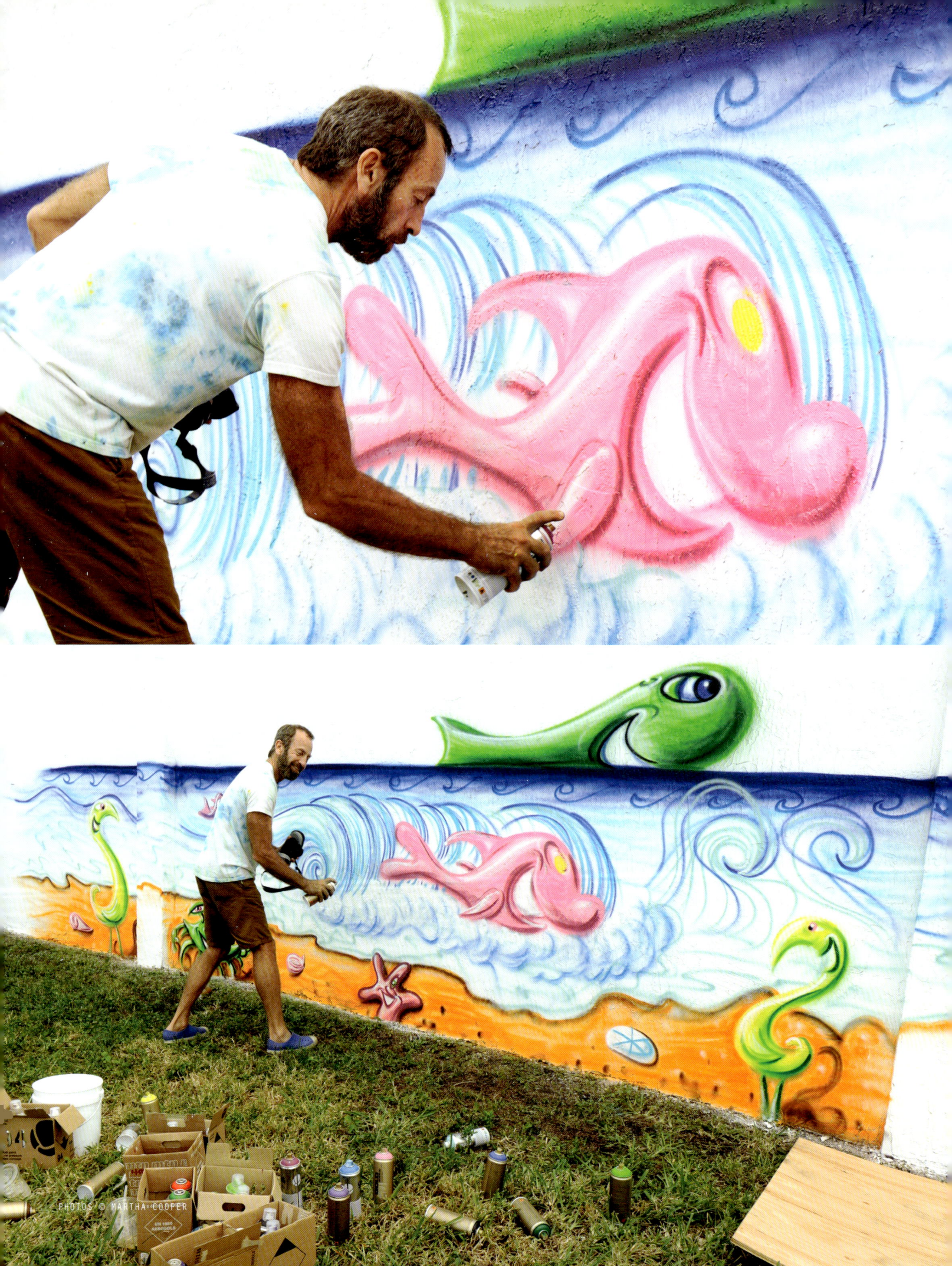

PHOTOS © MARTHA COOPER

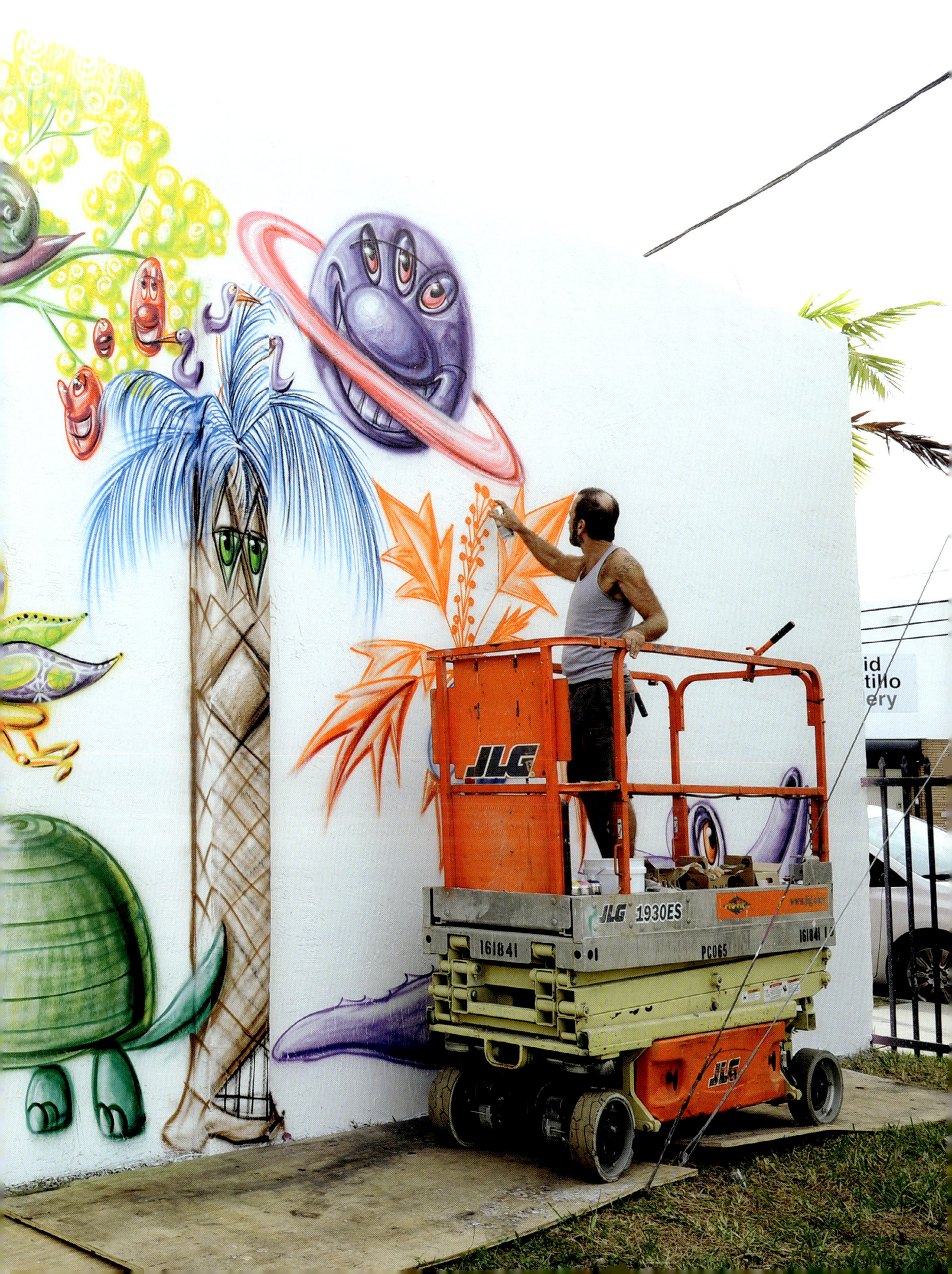

JLG
JLG 1930ES
161841
PC065

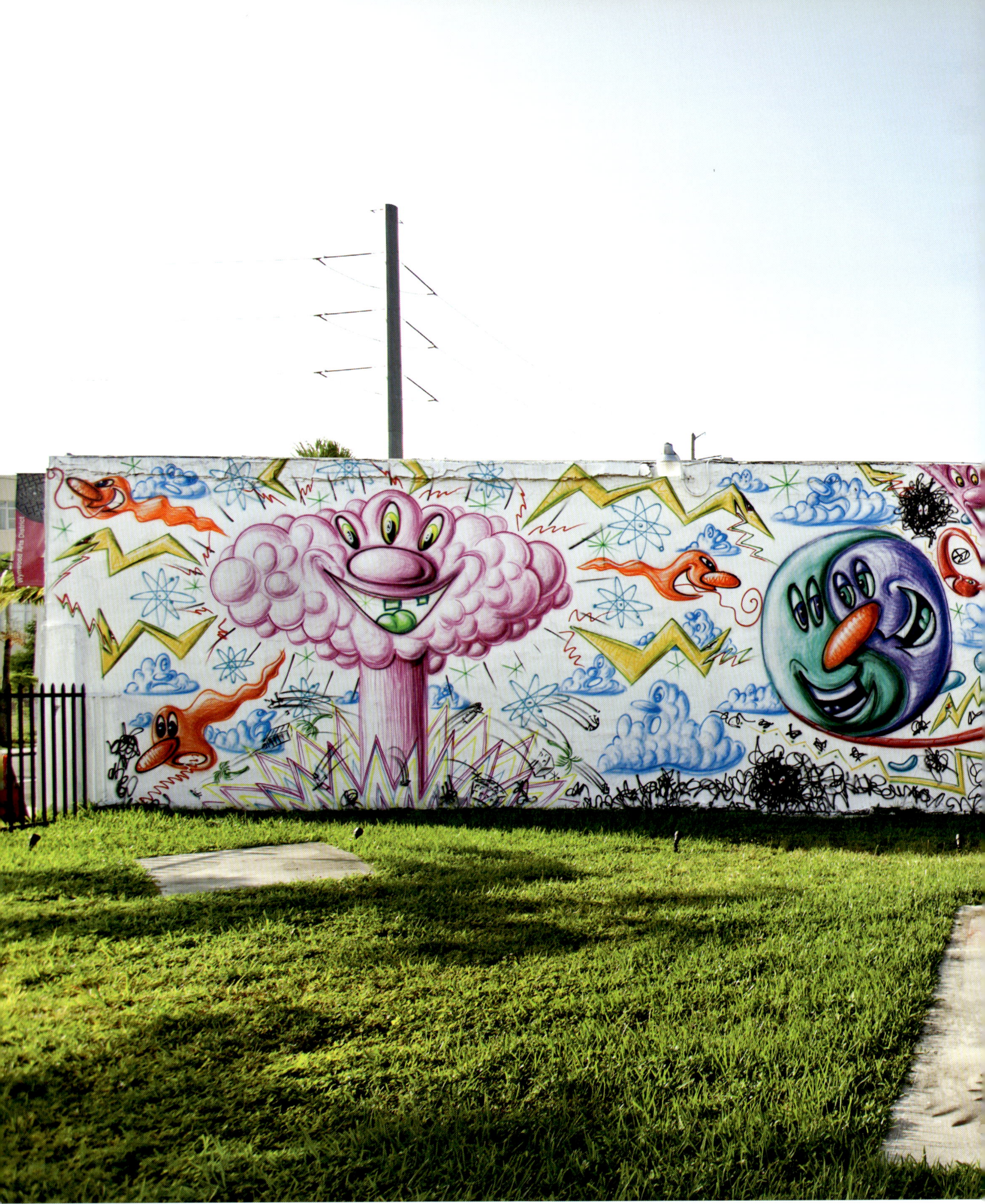

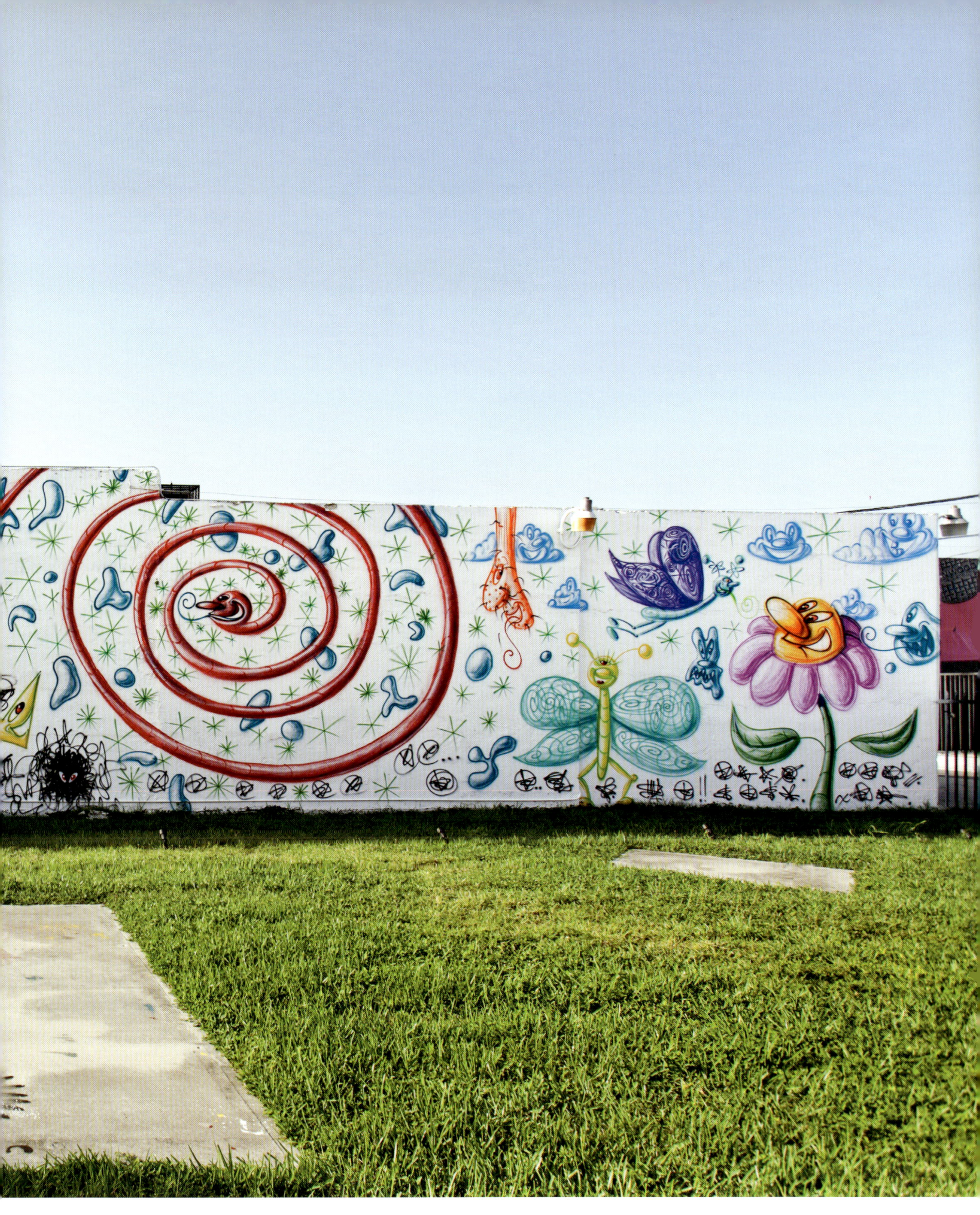

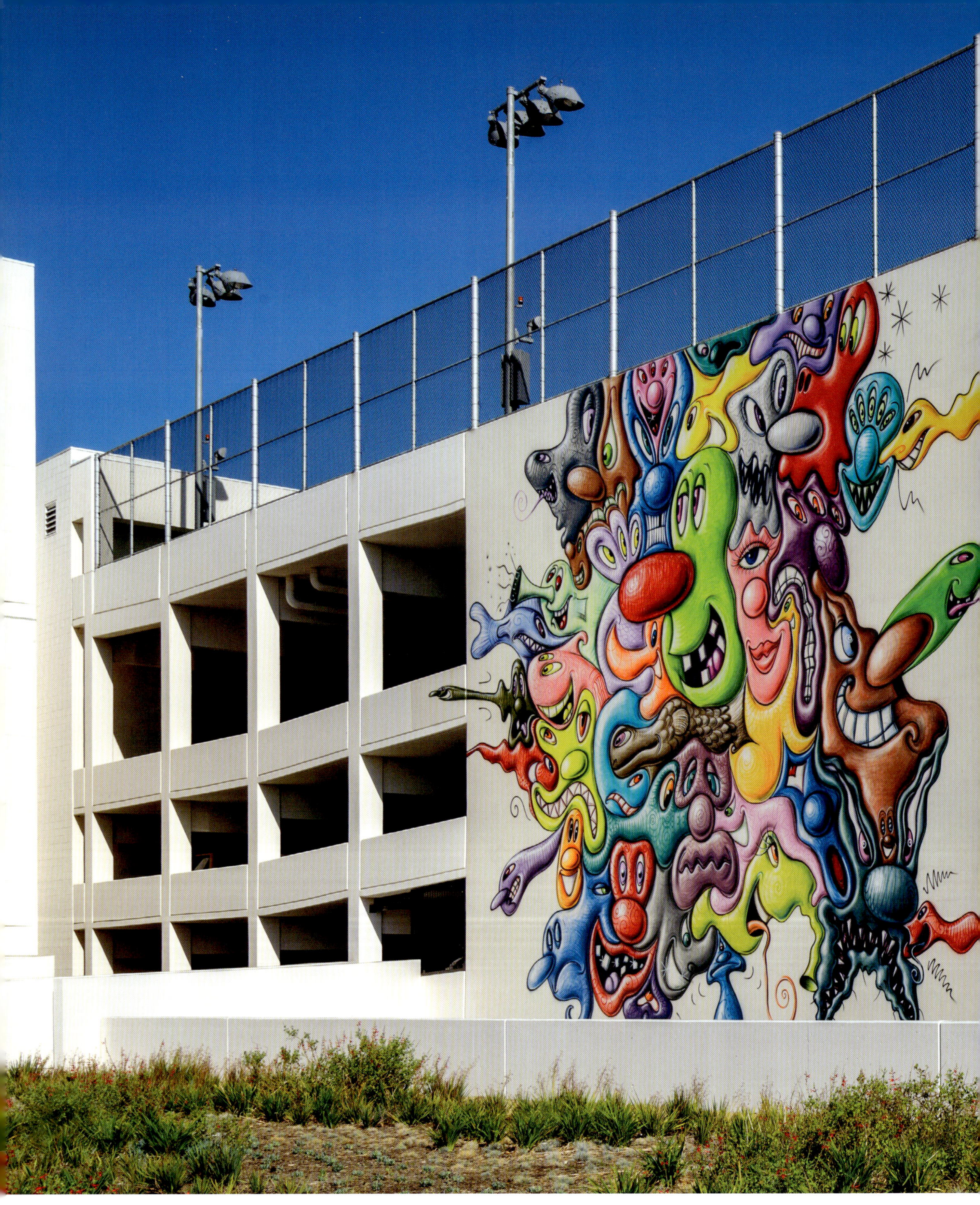

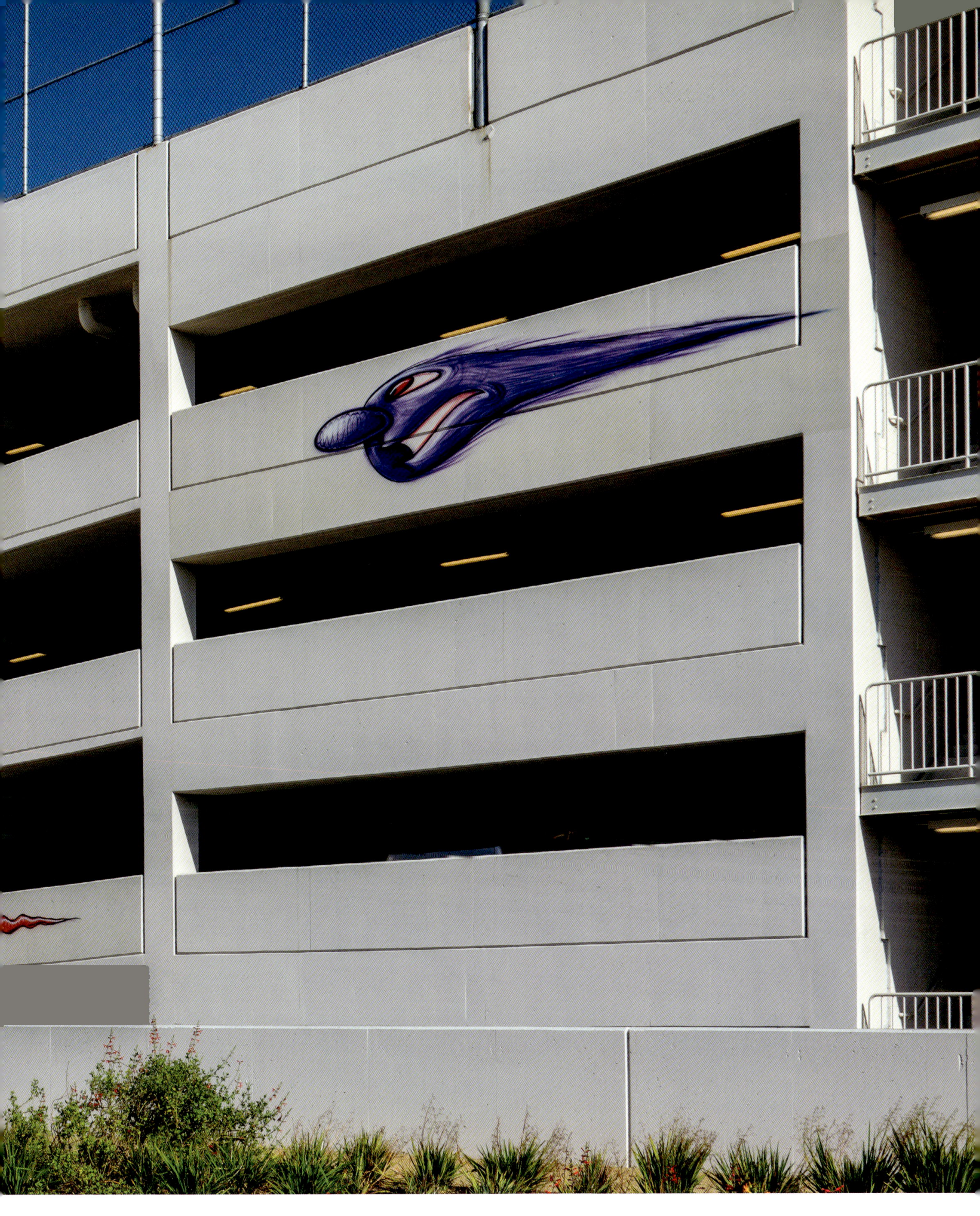

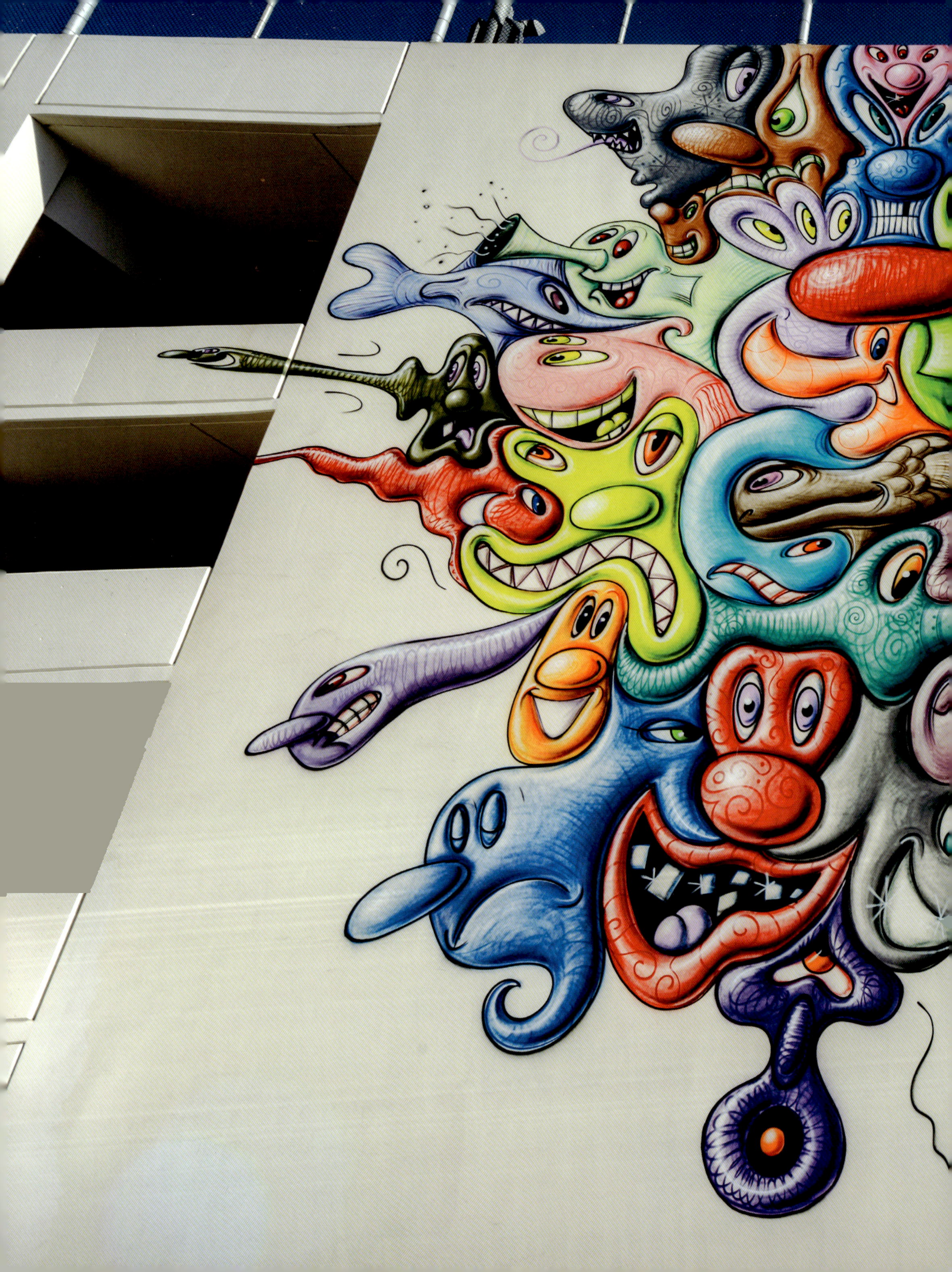

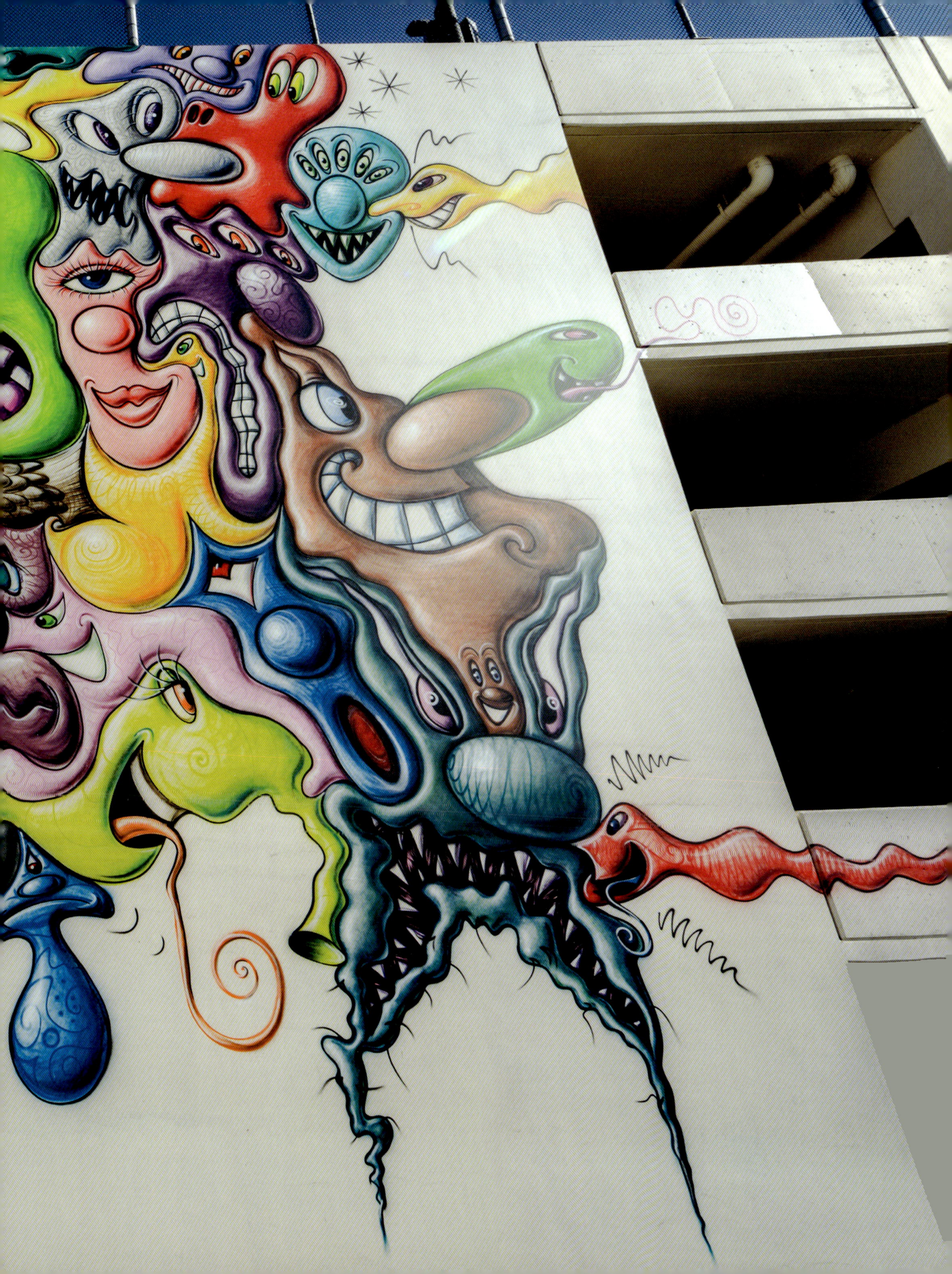

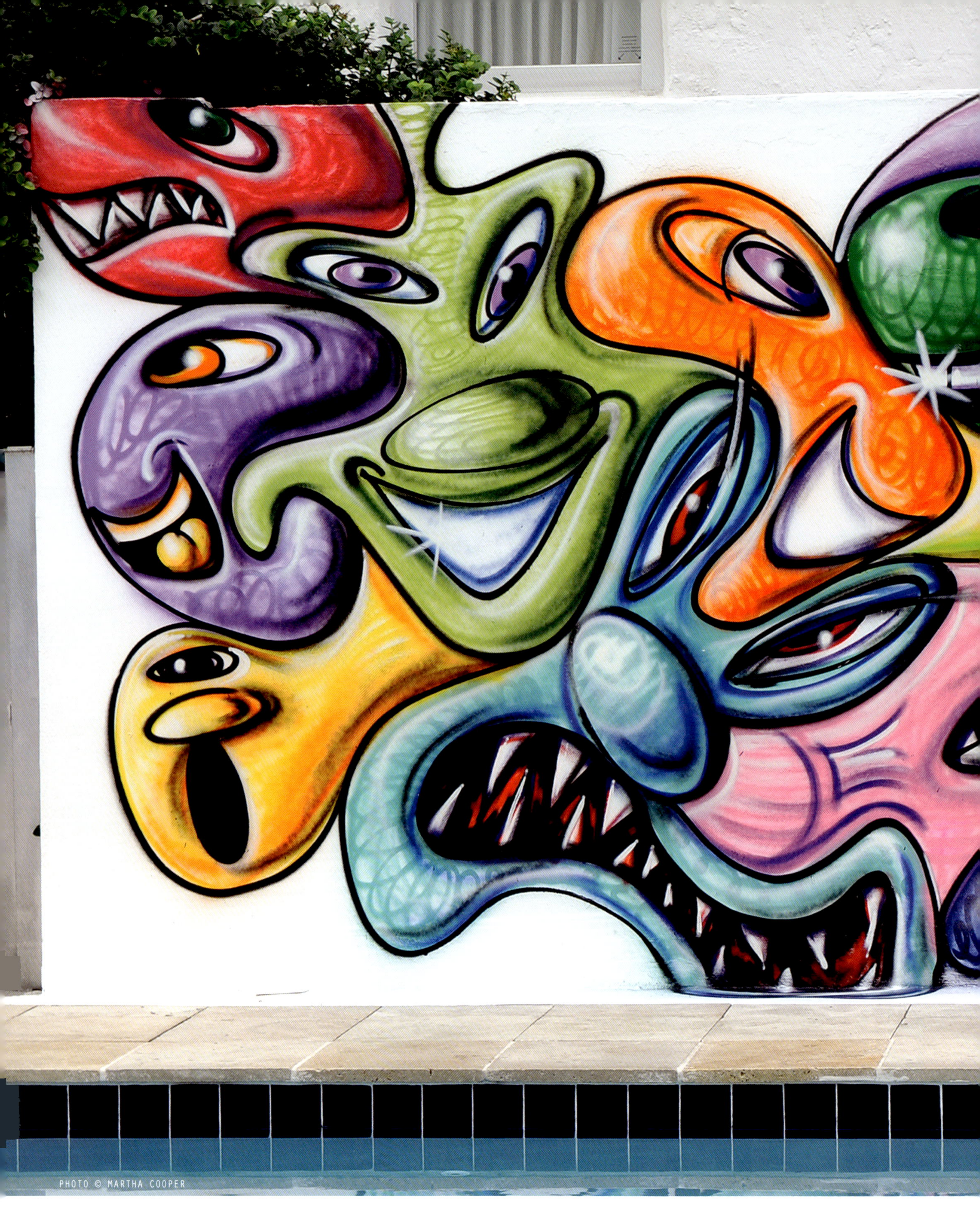

PHOTO © MARTHA COOPER

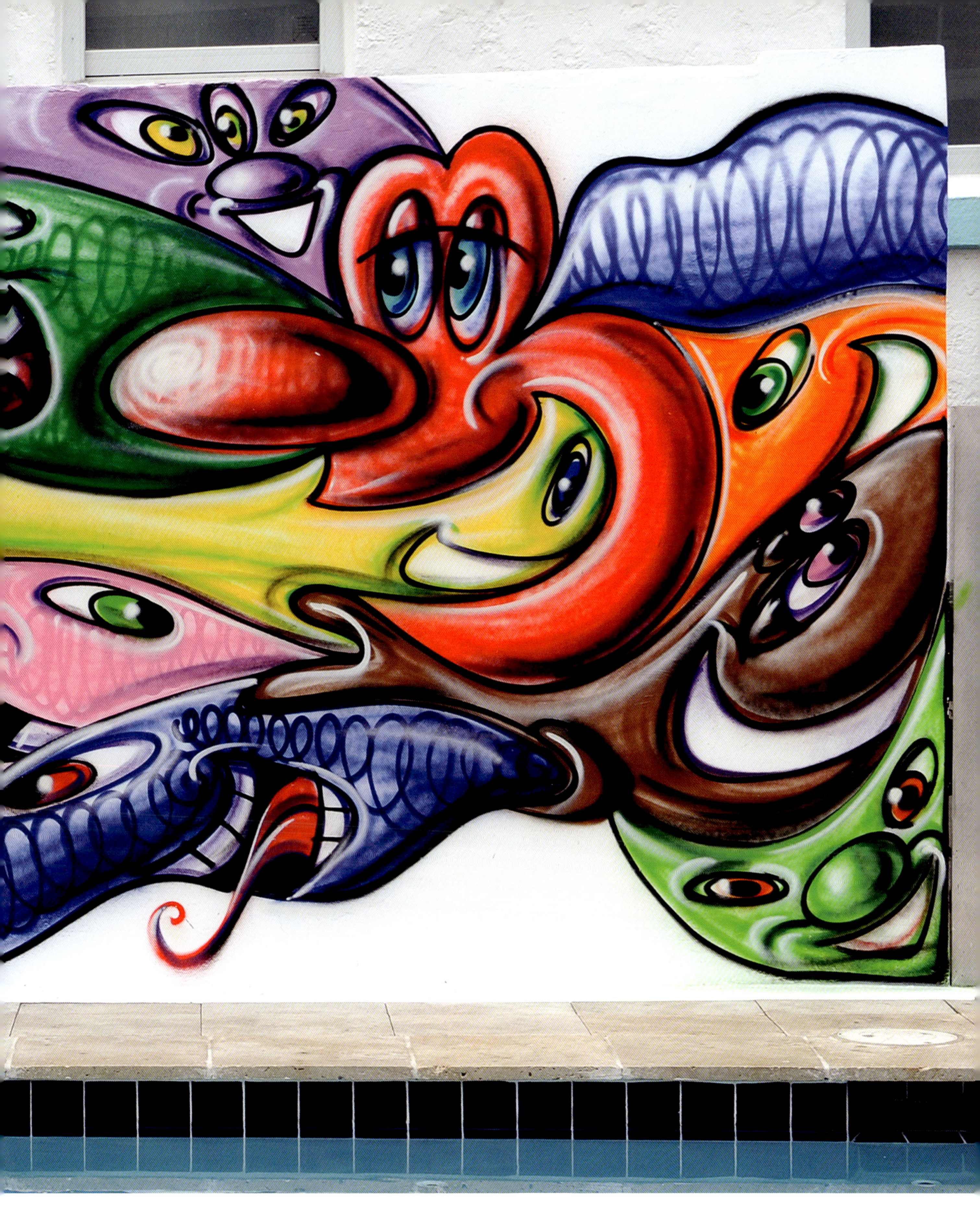

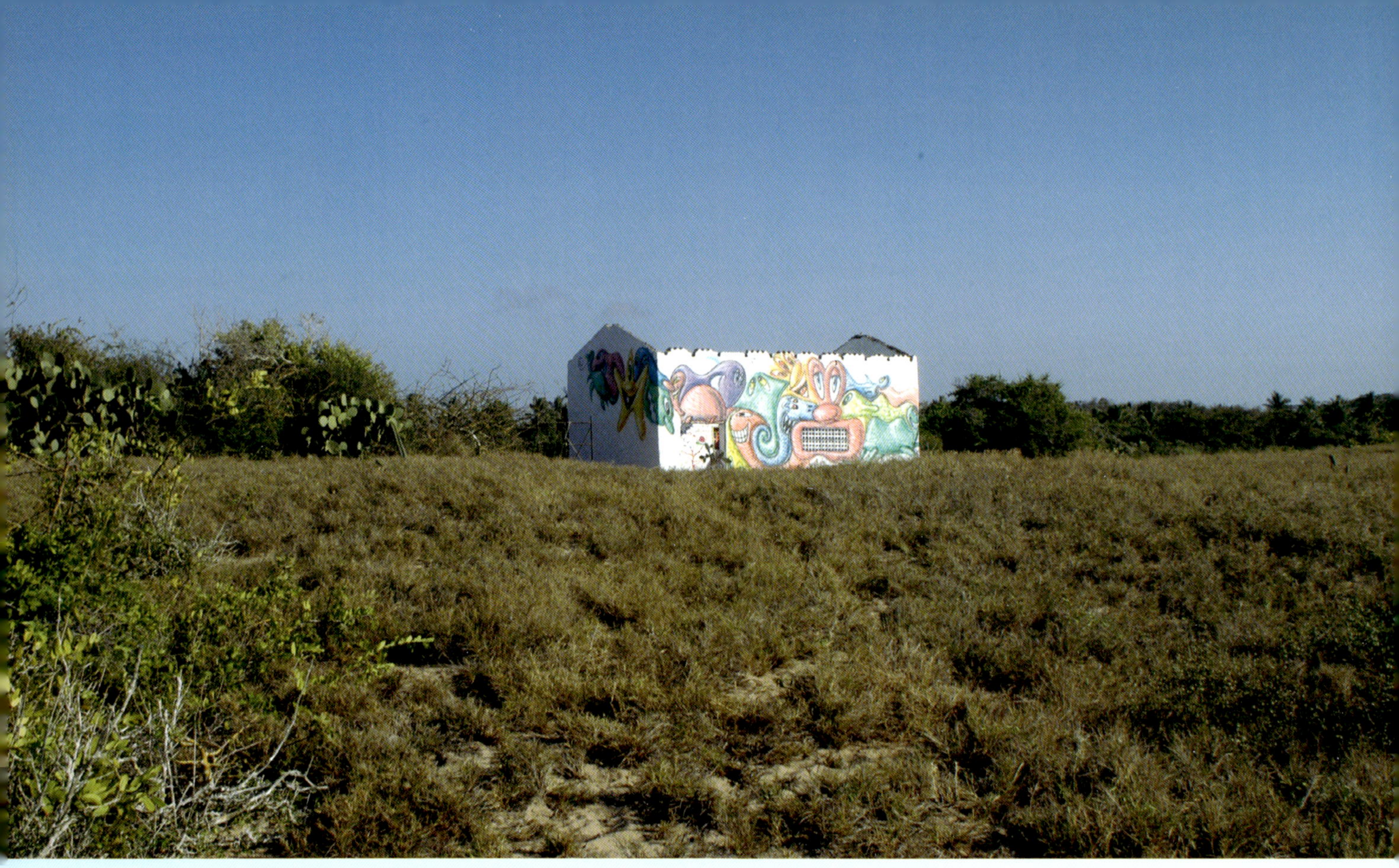

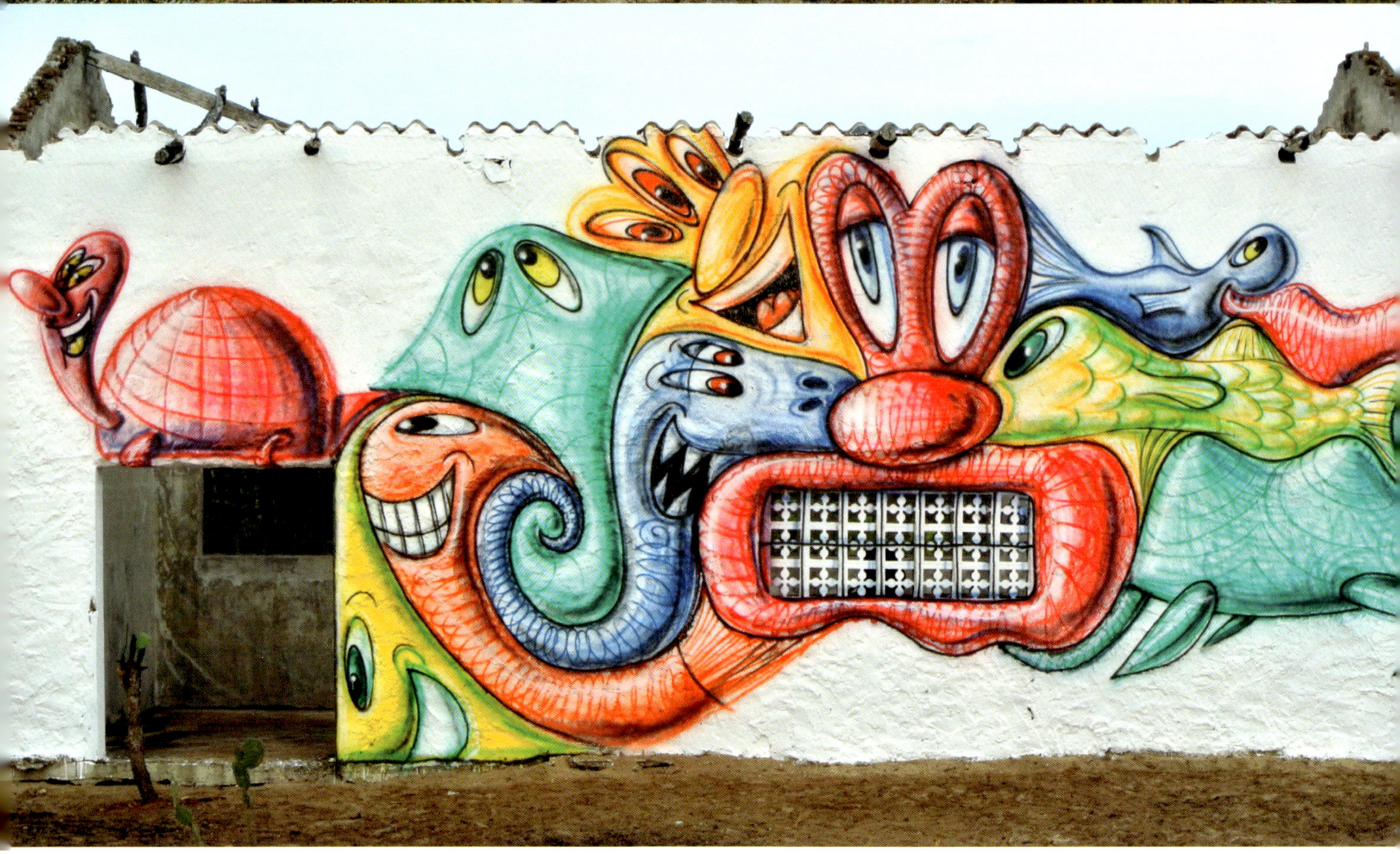

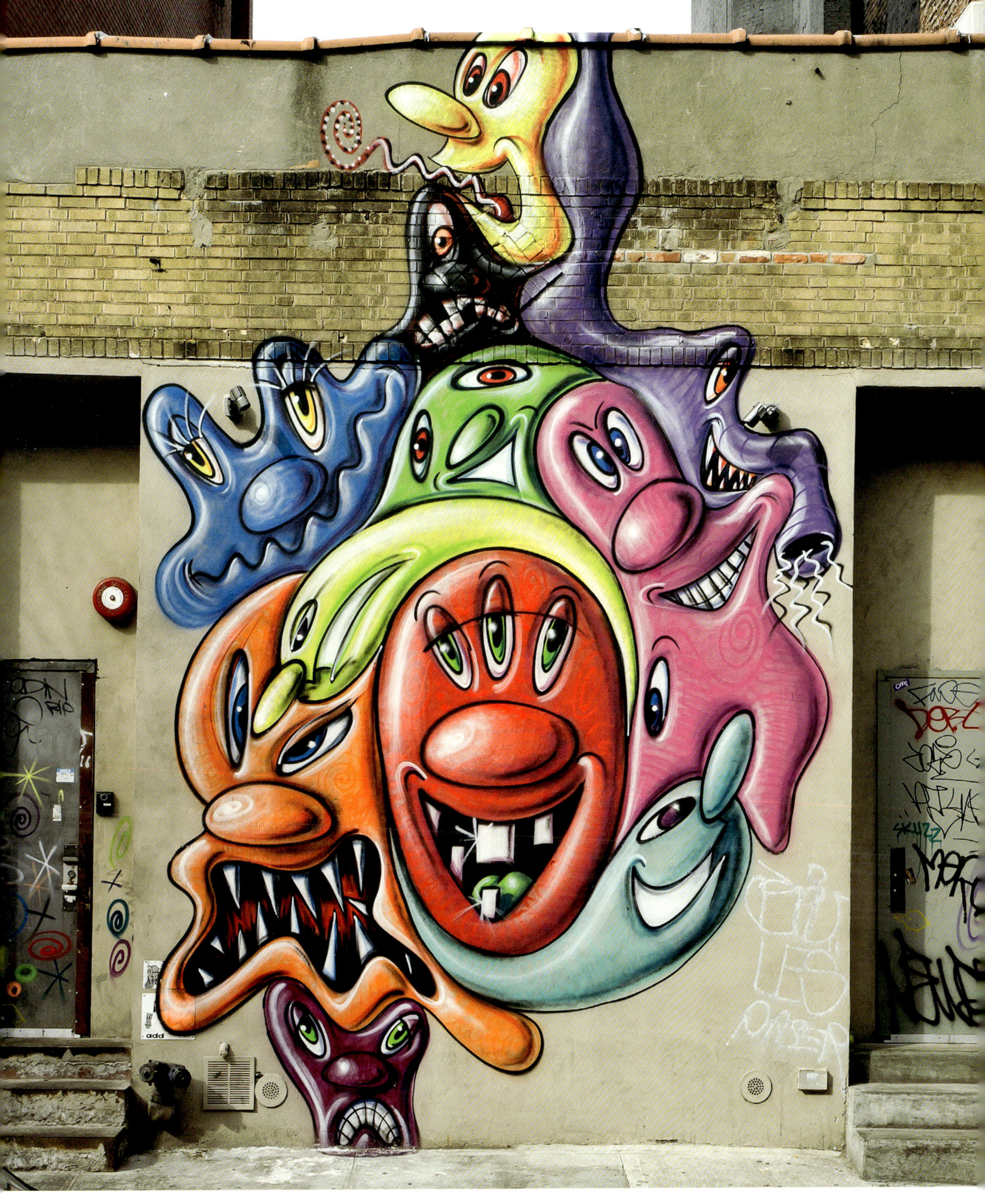

NORFOLK & STANTON CHUNKPACK / NEW YORK CITY 2012

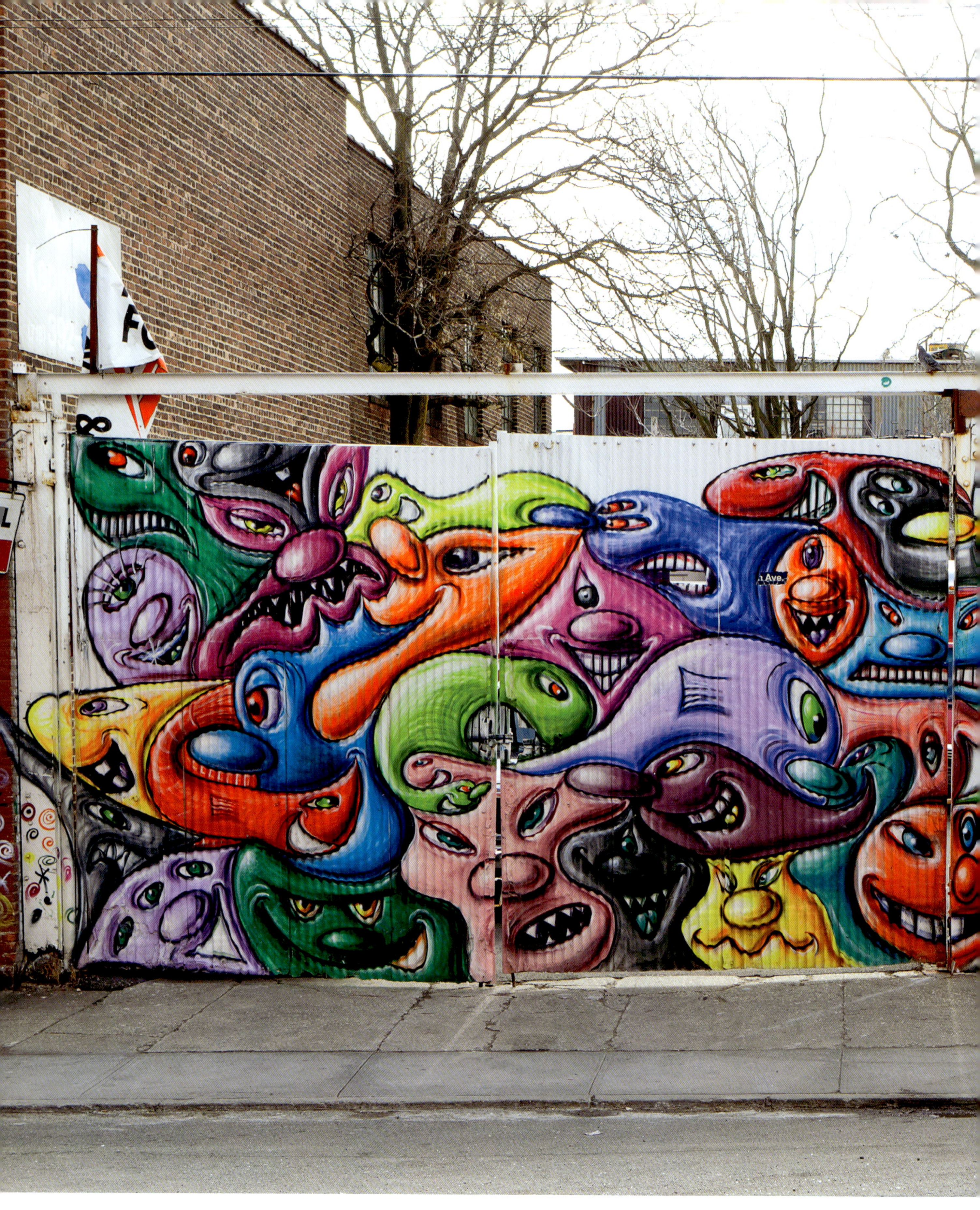

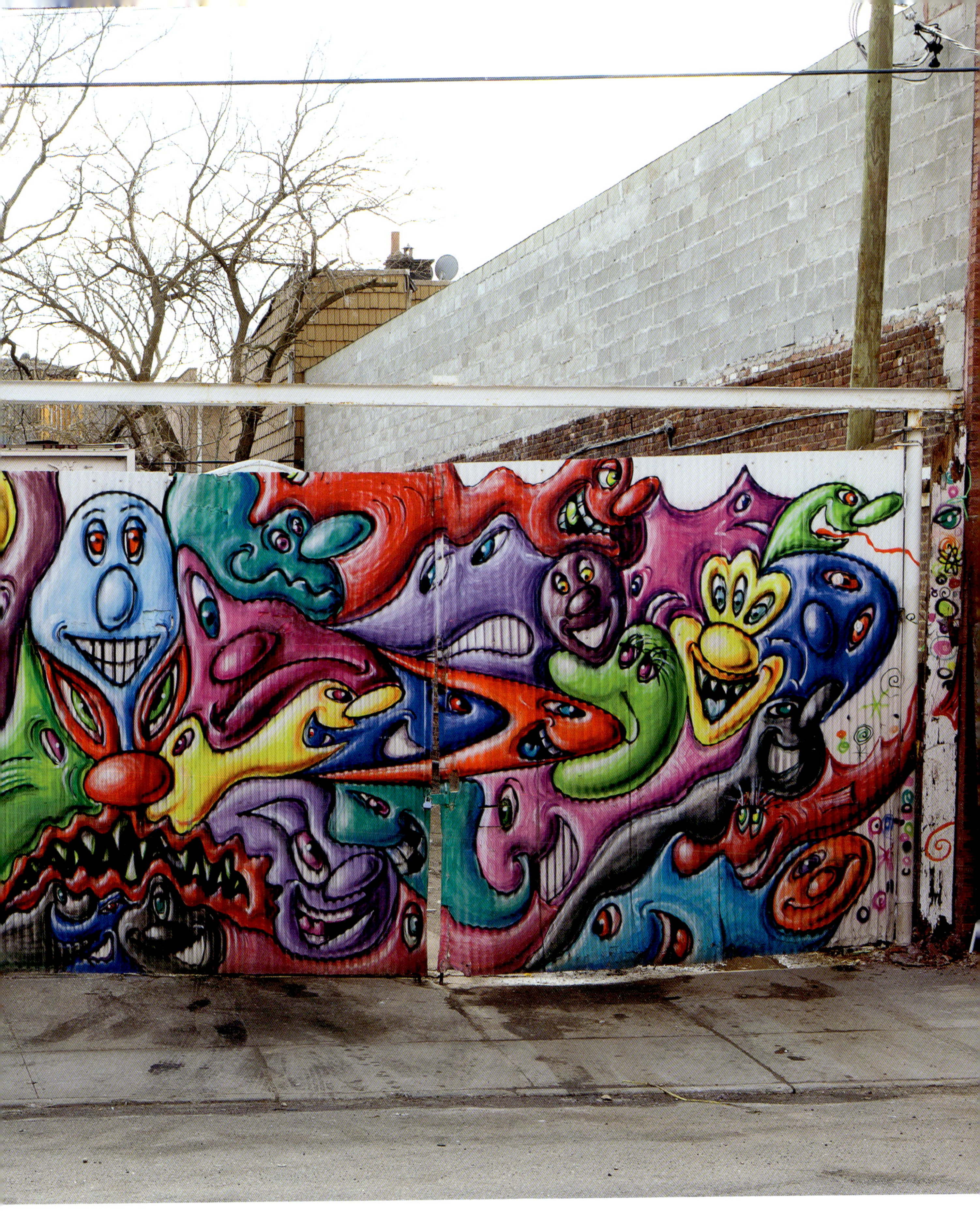

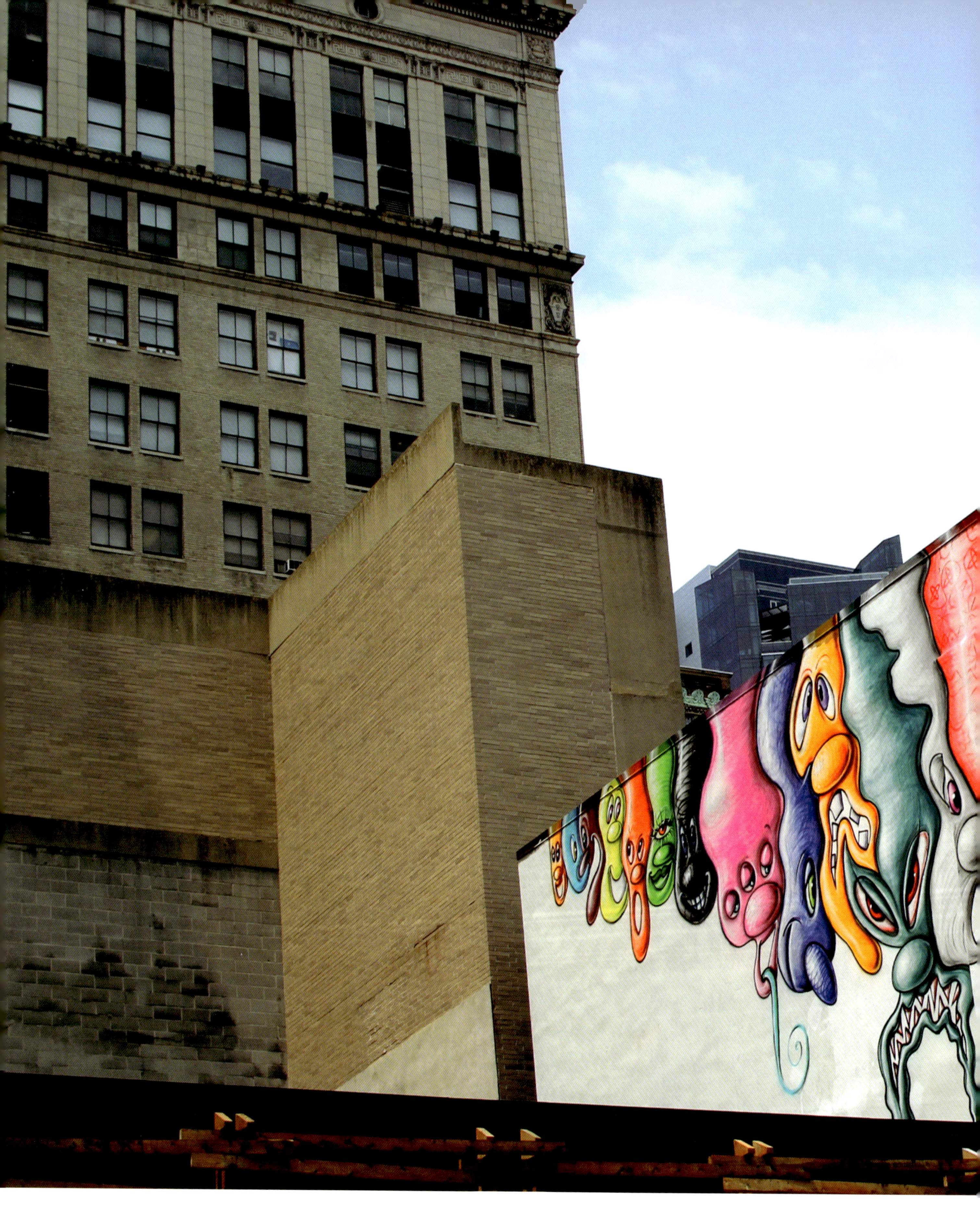

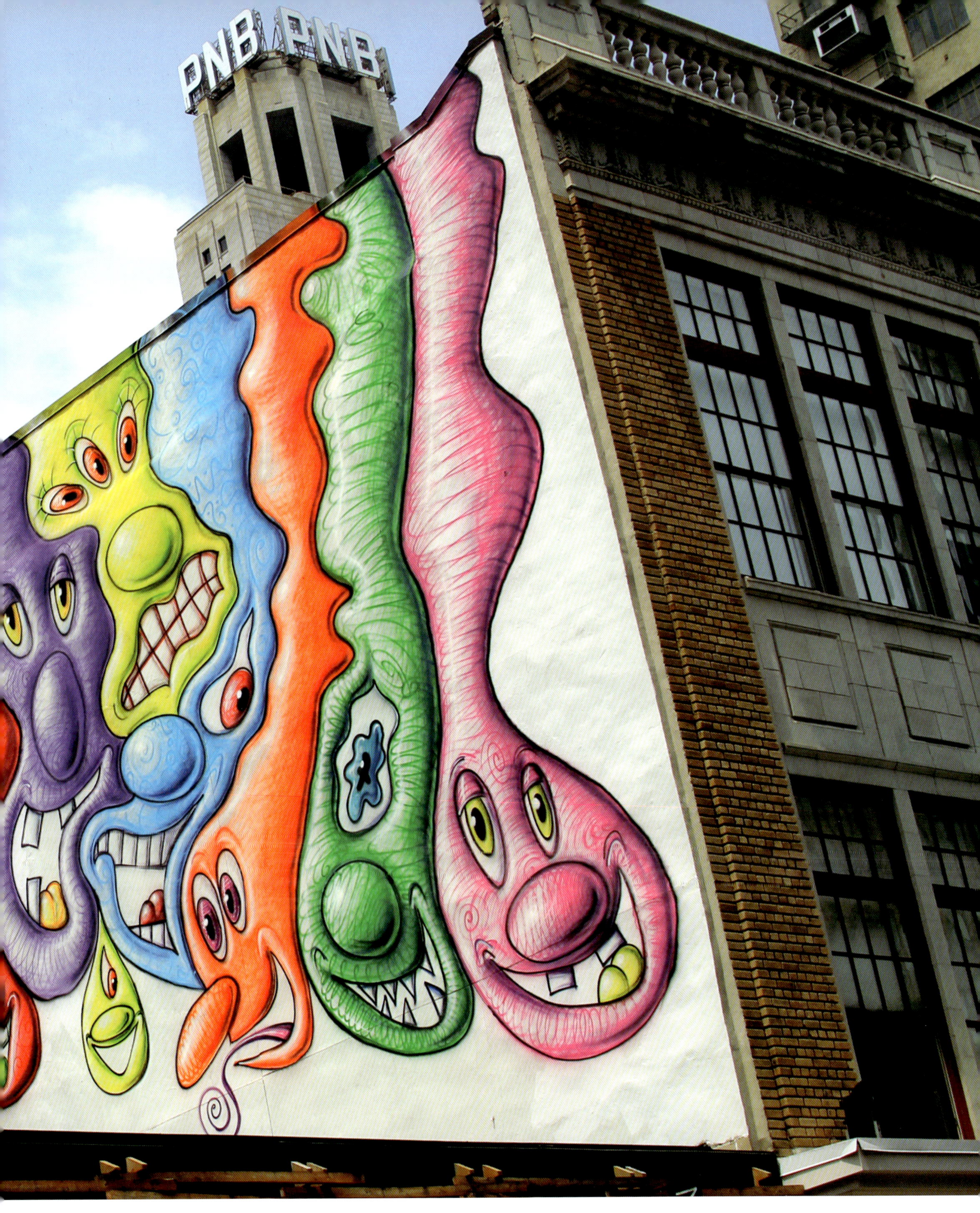
PNB PNB

ART IN THE STREETS

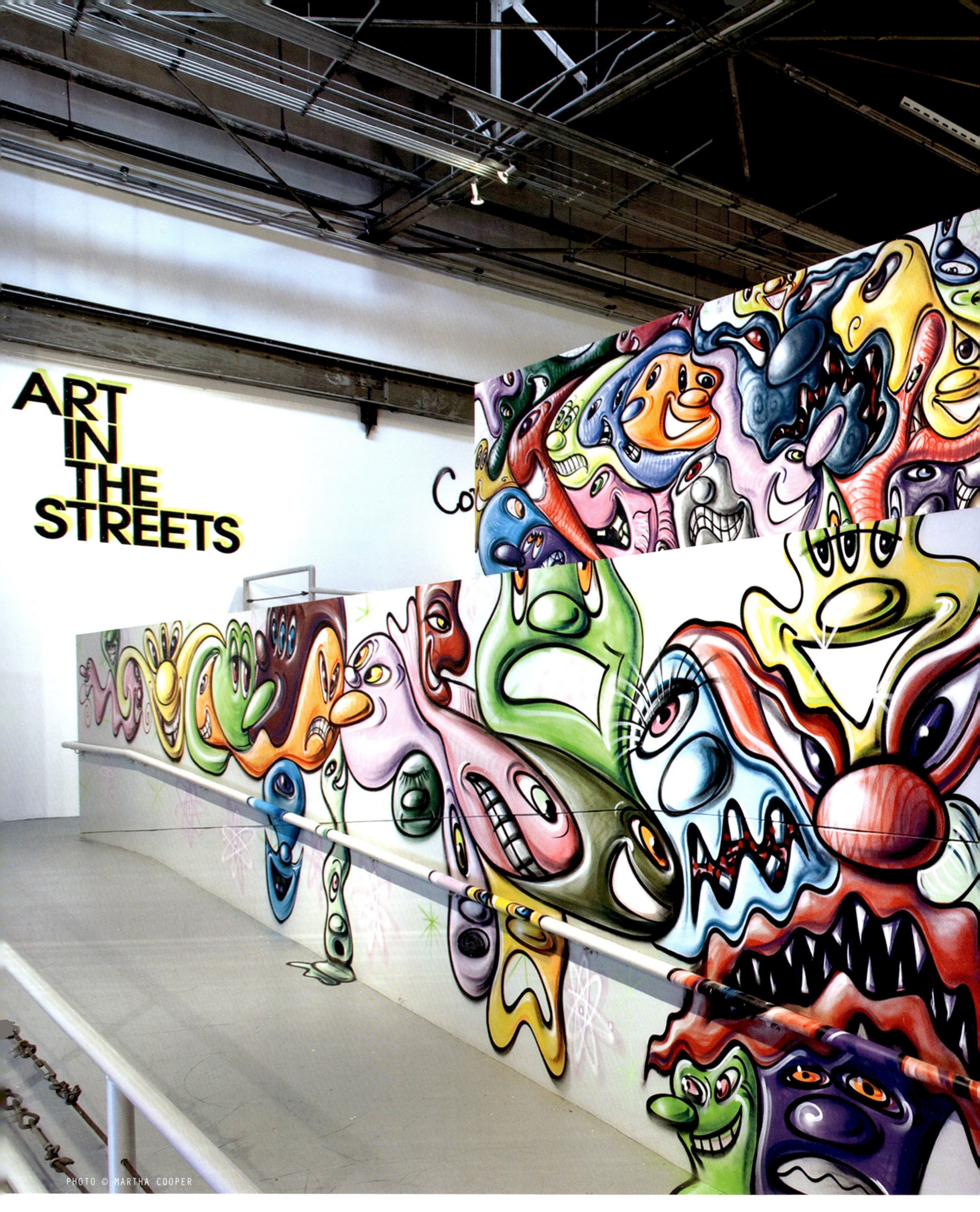

PHOTO © MARTHA COOPER

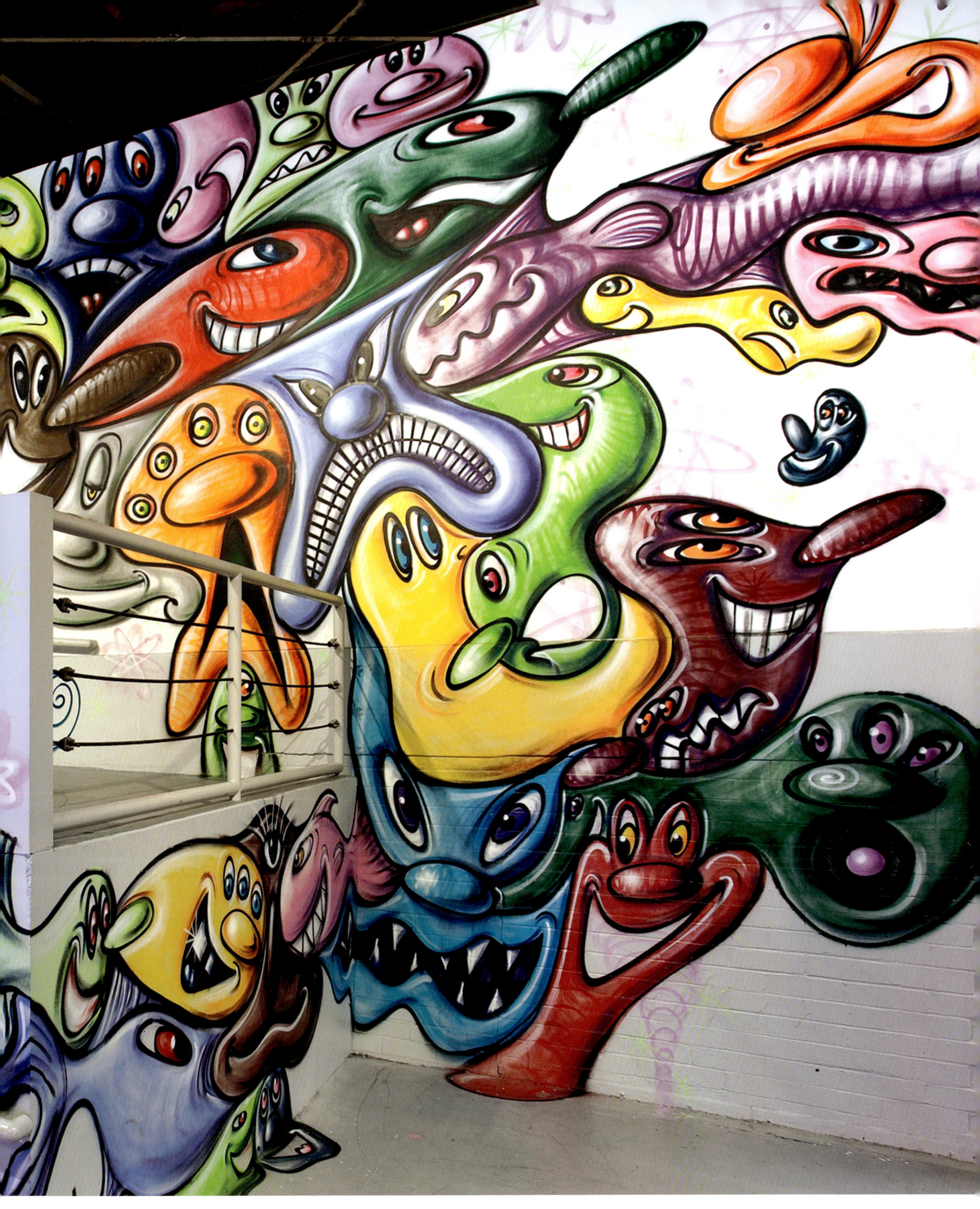

MOCA CHUNKPACK / ART IN THE STREETS - MOCA LA / LOS ANGELES 2010

KENNY SCHARF
KOLORS

ART DIRECTION
TONY ARCABASCIO

EDITORIAL DIRECTION
CLAIRE DARROW MOSIER

PHOTOGRAPHY
CHRIS MOSIER / P 5, 8-21, 42-45, 48-55, 57, 59-60, 89, 90-91
CHRISTOPHER BURKE STUDIOS / P 24-31
DAVID MORGAN / P 32-35, 38-41
JOSHUA WHITE / P 36-37, 46-47, 62, 82-85, 92-93
GENTLE GIANT STUDIOS / P 58
© MARTHA COOPER / P 66-79, 86-87, 94-95
MARK MARKIN / P 63
FILIPPO BRIGNONE / P 88

PUBLISHED ON THE OCCASION OF THE EXHIBITION
KENNY SCHARF / KOLORS
ON VIEW AT PAUL KASMIN GALLERY
515 WEST 27TH STREET, NEW YORK
APRIL 4- MAY 4, 2013

SPECIAL THANKS
TONY ARCABASCIO, IRVING BLUM, BETHANIE BRADY,
CLAIRE DARROW MOSIER, JEFFREY DEITCH, DAN CAMERON, PAUL KASMIN,
RICHARD MARSHALL, MARK MARKIN, CARLO MCCORMICK,
DAVE MORGAN, CHRIS MOSIER, & NICK OLNEY

The Standard

STANDARD PRESS
23 EAST 4TH STREET, 5TH FLOOR
NEW YORK CITY, NY 10003
WWW.STANDARDCULTURE.COM

DAMIANI

DAMIANI
VIA ZANARDI 376, BOLOGNA - ITALY
TEL: +39 051 6356811
FAX: +39 051 6347188
WWW.DAMIANIEDITORE.COM

ISBN# 978-88-6208-287-7

PRINTED IN MARCH 2013 BY GRAFICHE DAMIANI, ITALY

DISTRIBUTED IN THE UNITED STATES OF AMERICA BY
ARTBOOK | D.A.P.
155 SIXTH AVENUE
NEW YORK CITY, NY 10013
WWW.ARTBOOK.COM